TELL ME WHO I AM

A collection of essays on family, faith and identity

Compiled by DeNae Handy

STANSBURY HOUSE PUBLICATIONS

ISBN: 978-0615605722

Cover Art and Design: Jana Winters Parkin
Interior Art: Jana Winters Parkin
Interior Layout: Katie Wright

STANSBURY HOUSE PUBLICATIONS

www.stansburyhousepublications.com

TELL ME WHO I AM

Foreword

This is a collection of stories – stories one might hear while out strolling at *'that time of evening, when people sit on their porches, rocking gently and talking gently.'* James Agee's words evoke memories of my own childhood, summer nights when we lay on blankets under the stars as the grownups talked about the little things that were really the big things: work, raising families, enduring loss and learning to laugh again, holding on to even the tiniest thread of faith because letting go was unthinkable.

As dusk turned to dark and the grass cooled beneath us, we would, in pairs, take hold of the corners of our blankets and roll together until we resembled the twin babies I used to fold out of my grandmother's handkerchief. Now, wrapped and warm, we could listen to our parents and their friends share stories *'of nothing in particular,'* stories that told us who they were, and how they came to be there on that porch, on that evening, under those stars.

"I am little ladies with kerchiefed heads," Karen Burton writes, "and farmers who keep pigs. I am hard-working immigrants who toil in woolen mills and tend to my children after a long day. I am women who are devoted to family and culture. I am all of the people who have come before me."

They who 'come before me' leave stories in their wake, and their stories show me where I'm from. Held to the mirror of my own life, they reveal what I've become. They wrap themselves around me, weaving their threads into the fabric of my own stories.

And someday, when all of my stories are gathered in, perhaps they will 'tell me who I am.'

DeNae Handy

James Agee quotes from "Knoxville," Agee's introductory essay to his Pulitzer Prize-winning posthumous novel, A Death in the Family.

Karen Burton quote from her blog, "Kazzy's Ponderings," http://kazzysponderings.blogspot.com

Contents

SECTION TWO

Unplanned by Me

SECTION FOUR

In the Hour of their Taking Away

SECTION FIVE

Master-gardener of his Soul

SECTION ONE

"Humor is emotional chaos remembered in tranquility."

James Thurber

All We, Like Sheep

DeNae Handy

Easter 2006 found my family in the Peruvian Andes. How it ever thought to look there is a true mystery; all we could remember was that one minute we were playing "¿Quién es mas macho?" with an Incan bartender, and the next we were sniffing llama toes.

Ha! I kid. The only drinking game my family plays is the one where you eat a fistful of Mentos, drink a jumbo extra-grande Diet Coke, and then watch each other's heads explode. Makes for a great Family Home Evening activity.

We were working with a humanitarian group in the little village of Salkantay, Peru, which is one mile above and 200 years behind Cuzco.

There is no more beautiful place on the earth than Salkantay, Peru. Those Andes don't mess around with gentle slopes and rolling foot-hills. They shoot straight up into the stratosphere—and beyond, it seems—to the 14,000 foot elevation where the village is situated, thumbing their majestic noses at wimpy ideas like gravity. They're green and precipitous, and, in every possible sense of the word, breathtaking. This is the only place I've ever visited where you order oxygen from the hotel desk and a bellman brings it to your room. For a larger tip, he'll strap a bicycle pump to your face and re-inflate your lungs.

Our group spent a week or so helping the villagers with a variety of projects, including building a greenhouse, constructing a running water system, and introducing the little Peruvian children to the modern, transcendent wonders of Spicy Cheetos. Many of the villagers were descendants of the Inca and only spoke Ketchua. A few spoke Spanish as well. None spoke English. Yet it was great to see our kids working side-by-side with the locals, communicating with sign language and stick-in-the-dirt drawings and the kind of laughter you get when you realize the table you just spent an hour building has three legs pointing south and one due west.

The experience was life changing. I have forever after looked at my children with different eyes.

One morning, however, we arrived at the village to learn that we'd be participating in a new project. The village was raising a special variety of sheep. I'm not sure which variety, exactly. I think it was the "Woolicus Stupidus," but I could be lying. It was hoped that these sheep, if kept healthy, would provide high-quality wool which could be used to make blankets, clothing, and other products which the villagers would take into Cuzco and sell. The impoverished residents of Salkantay pinned a lot of their hopes for future prosperity on those sheep.

A big part of keeping the sheep healthy long enough to realize a return on the village's investment was immunizing them. I couldn't tell you what kinds of diseases sheep are likely to get (*mad cow?*) but we were nonetheless given the job of getting them vaccinated.

It should probably be noted here that, to a man, not a single member of our humanitarian expedition knew the first thing about sheep. Zip. I'm not sure any could even spell the word 'sheep'. Nevertheless, possessed of the hubris that is the downfall of tourists everywhere, we trotted up the hillside to assume our duties as Sheep Herding & Immunization Technology Specialists, or for short, umm . . . well, never mind.

The first thing we noticed after regaining consciousness (*after all, we were three miles above sea level*) was that there were no sheep in the pasture. There was, technically, no *pasture* in the pasture. It was more along the lines of a grassy wall, which climbed at a gentle 175-degree angle until it met with an ascending cliff that rose so aggressively "up" that it appeared to loop back on the geometric continuum, qualifying more as an inverted "down."

This cliff was where the sheep were grazing—evidently affixed to the mountain by Velcro—and keeping them company was a herd of llamas.

Also on that vertiginous mountainside were some of the local shepherds, who, upon noticing our group sucking wind and collapsing like fish on a boat bottom, began to direct both the sheep and the llamas toward the pasture. I can't really describe how they did it, but somehow the shepherds managed to separate the llamas from the sheep, dispatching the llamas toward the village and leaving the sheep—and their victims—to their respective fates.

One of the men instructed our group on the finer points of immunizing sheep. It seemed we were to first herd the sheep into an adobe pen, where the local toughs would single out individual animals, and, using a complex formula known as "guessing," would call out to us, the volunteer sheep-dopers, the amount of medicine the sheep required. After the medicine had been administered, another batch of idiots—er, I mean *humanitarians*—would paint the heads of the now-vaccinated sheep with red goo, indicating that they were finished, and then the sheep would be free to leave the pen.

Sounds simple enough, right?

Oh. My. Word.

Let it here be observed, when the Lord referred to His children as "sheep" He was not paying them a compliment. It was a toss-up as to which creatures on that hillside were more brainless, more stubborn, more skittish, goofy and easily distracted – the human volunteers or those blasted sheep. The pasture and the pen were maybe fifty yards away from each other, forty-nine of those yards pointing straight down. We could simply have picked up the sheep and dropped them into the pen if we could have caught them. But it took us nearly an hour of sheer buffoonery to do the job.

First, we thought we could just "holler" the sheep down the hill: "Go, sheep! Go on! Go, sheep, go!" We sounded like we'd been scripted by Dr. Seuss. The sheep, naturally, heeded our counsel by running in a circle and pooing.

Persuasion having failed, we accepted that we were going to have to terrify them into cooperating. We removed various jackets and hats, then jogged and flailed and breathed out threatenings against those cursed sheep and their posterity to the third and fourth generations. The sheep responded by assuming individual trajectories and running in what was now forty different circles and bleating revolutionary slogans at their tormentors. And pooing some more.

Clearly, fear wasn't going to work. Next on the agenda, then, was an attempt at creating an inspirational movie moment by kidnapping a few of the lambs and carrying them toward the pen, confident that their mothers would follow along out of powerful maternal instinct. Oh, the mileage we would get out of this object lesson!

Unfortunately, sheep don't watch inspirational movies. Instead, they interpreted our act of collecting all the lambs as an offer of free babysitting, and celebrated their new-found liberty by frolicking in a general anti-pen direction and, of course, pooing.

The hillside was becoming a slippery slope of unmentionable terrors for us gringos, who were wearing our "old" sneakers for the job. This meant we'd essentially strapped rubber ice skates to our feet and were trying to keep from falling into what you get when you combine a stressed-out sheep with a grass-intensive brunch.

Strangely, we had the best luck when we simply hid from the sheep. "They're getting nervous," we reasoned. "Give them some time to settle down. Let 'em think we've lost interest. Then we'll break out the tranquilizer darts." Sure enough, a few sheep gravitated toward the pen, and once we got three or four contained, the rest, as sheep are wont to do, followed along.

Now it was time for the wrestling match, wherein the local herdsmen would quite literally pick up a sheep in a position reminiscent of the Heimlich maneuver, and shout "Dos!" or "Cuatro!" which told the volunteers how many cc's of medicine that sheep needed.

Meanwhile, we were either filling syringes with anywhere from two to five cc's of a milky substance, or handing them to others, who then rushed over to the Heimlich-ed sheep and squirted the medicine into its mouth.

Yeah, that went well.

Not knowing that this stuff could mean the difference between good health and poor—perhaps between surviving the wet Andean winter or not—the sheep had no interest in cooperating with the immunizers. They spit. They thrashed. They pulled out shivs and menaced the other sheep. They mouthed off and stomped up to their rooms.

As if that weren't enough, once the medicine that wasn't all over the volunteer's shoes was in the sheep's mouth, the volunteer had to massage its throat to force the sheep to swallow. The immunizer would then shout "Paint!" and another volunteer rushed over to brush red dye on the sheep's head. The sheep was finally released to go its way, only to be as obstinate and stupid about exiting the pen as it had been about entering.

From start to finish, it was one big exercise in coercion and, at times, sheer, teeth-gritting determination not to be out-maneuvered by a 150-pound helium balloon in a wool sweater. Those sheep did everything they could to reject what was being offered to them. They were short-sighted and temperamental and even aggressively determined to remain unprotected, exposed, and vulnerable to whatever disease or discomfort lay ahead. They had to be led, pushed, and threatened. For some, it took several attempts from several well-stomped laborers to finally get the job done. But by the end of the day, every one of those silly sheep bore on its head the symbol of its renewed health and brighter future.

I have often reflected on that morning. I've thought about sheep and people and how difficult it can sometimes be to do something good and necessary and even life-saving for others. About the kind of vision and effort it takes to call and contain creatures that might otherwise never pay a lick of attention to what you do or say or want for them.

I've considered the love poured into the healing of all mortality's pain, including—especially—the healing of broken hearts, and the mark set upon those hearts when they have been made whole by the Master Physician.

And mostly, I've learned a little more about the Good Shepherd, who on another hillside on another Easter, reclaimed His sheep and, one by one, anointed their heads with salvation, inviting them to forever lie down in the green pastures of eternal life.

All we, like sheep, have gone astray. But we hear the voice of the Shepherd, who knows us, has borne our griefs, carried our sorrows, and graven us on the palms of His hands.

And we follow Him.

Beyond Baby Tenderlove

Jana Winters Parkin

One Christmas, my younger sister and I begged and pleaded for the only toy on the market we wanted that year: Baby Tenderlove. Somehow the name alone invoked every maternal sentiment in our chubby little preschool bodies, and we longed to snuggle that sweet baby doll more than anything else we could imagine. We were thrilled on Christmas morning when we each opened our very own Baby Tenderlove, ready to rock, feed and put to sleep.

I didn't feel that way again until I was pregnant with my first. As the months of expectancy went by, I found myself longing once again for Baby Tenderlove—not the plastic doll, of course, but my own fleshy baby I could dote on and love the way I did when I was five. Dreams of quiet snuggling, humming and rocking to sleep, and deep, tranquil tenderness were in the forefront of my consciousness.

The baby came, and suddenly I woke up. I got many serene moments with Baby Tenderlove. But I also got "Baby Cries All Night." I tried desperately to feed "Baby Hurts to Nurse." Then I discovered "Baby Makes a Mess," who generated more dirty laundry than both its parents combined. There was also a bath-time version: "Baby Slippery When Wet." Then newer models arrived: "Baby Projectile Vomit" and "Baby Exploding Diaper." If I were writing a marketing campaign for a newborn, it might go something like: "Eight toys in one . . . some frightening and dangerous." I'd also add: "providing even the wildest thrill seeker with a heart-pounding emotional rollercoaster."

And it gets better, because "Baby Tenderlove" also grows up. It morphs into such creatures as "Toddler Destructo Unit" and "Kid Never, Ever Mind" . . . and even "Teenage Mutant Ninja Hormones."

I'm not the only one who was disillusioned in this scenario. I'm sure Baby Tenderlove expected to be born to Mama Tenderlove. Yes, I expected to *be* "Mama Tenderlove." I also thought I'd be a cross between Mary Poppins, Maria von Trapp, and Olivia Walton. Instead, once in a while I was Wicked Stepmother (*push buttons to hear her wretched voice!*), and often Distracted Working Mother (*bang head on counter to get her attention*).

But then there's a whole other toy box called Serendipity . . . sweet, unexpected surprises. For example, I was not prepared for the wonderfulness that is "Baby Heaven Scent." Ah, what would I give to bury my nose in the neck of a newborn! Also, I was completely caught off-guard, over and over again, by "Baby Giggle Magic." There aren't sufficient words to describe the joy of a baby's belly laugh.

Now, when I see our son attending college, tall, confident and handsome, knocking not just addiction, but also the academic world with his astronomic GPA; our daughter in the throes of high school, forming friendships, wrangling signs of first romance, and wantonly signing up for various sports teams, unafraid to make a fool of herself; and our youngest running off the field, all sweat and smiles, rinsing his dishes without being asked, sitting close enough to touch when we read together at night; when I step back and look past the messy details, one salient emotion is always strongest when everything settles: Tender love.

Un-Coaching

Chris Clark

S ome time ago, I was approached by a well-known blogger to write a post on the subject of "What Men Can Do to Help Their Wives Through Labor." This blogger seemed to believe that because my wife has successfully labored and delivered five babies, I must know the secret to stopping the screaming, or of making the baby come out easier, or how pushing the "call" button in just the right way will bring a nurse to the room more quickly.

I was surprised that this blogger expected me to know anything of this, as she happened to be my sister. She knew that our Lamaze classes were thirteen years ago, and that all I remembered from them was that the husband was supposed to get up in his wife's face and count. I've since learned that this is not such a good idea.

With my only suggestion proven one-hundred-percent wrong during our first childbirth experience, I concluded that I would be more effective in giving advice to men if I focused on giving pointers about what not to do while your wife is trying to have a baby.

Believe it or not, fellas, labor and delivery are not about us. I know you took your little classes, and that there is a better-than-average chance that this baby is yours, but still, this isn't your moment to call the shots and make "helpful" comments. Mostly, you need to be present, positive, and accept whatever demands are made of you.

Did I say "demands?" I meant "reasonable requests."

These reasonable requests may include "please hold my hand and let me squeeze yours for support," or possibly "please turn the channel, because "Two and a Half Men" just came on, and now the baby is afraid to come out."

You should know that all of my children were born in good, old-fashioned hospitals. I know women make many different birthing choices, and that these days, anything goes as along as the baby eventually emerges. I respect that, but I confess that hospital deliveries are all I know, so I'm of very little help to husbands whose wives choose to give birth in a hayloft or on a bobsled. Just take whichever of my non-suggestions fit your birthing plan. I wish you the best of luck.

FOOD:

Don't even think about it. Ever. Since a pregnant woman is essentially hungry all the time, it's likely your wife went into labor starving. It's also likely she won't be permitted to eat during labor because … well, it's gross, so I won't go into it. (*Honestly, I don't know why she can't eat. I just assume that "it's gross" covers all the dos and don'ts of childbirth.*)

So Rule #1: Don't bring a bag full of Wendy's burgers and snarf them down while your wife hungers and dilates. I get it; it's a waiting game. You're hungry, possibly bored. But guess what, sporto? If she doesn't eat, neither do you. And if your wife lovingly suggests that you should go eat, then you must look at her quizzically and say, "Really? Are you sure? Because . . . um . . . really?"

At this point you have a 50/50 chance of doing it right. I can't advise beyond that.

MUSIC:

I learned in Lamaze class that singing a special song during labor can be a beautiful shared experience between husband and wife. This concept was presented in a video, wherein a man and his wife—who, of course, was in labor—were in the shower together, soaping each other's backs. This sounds really dodgy, but it couldn't have been, because we were watching this movie in Pleasant Grove, Utah. This alone guarantees that the film was respectfully and modestly shot, and that no one will ever win an Oscar for it.

Anyway, this couple was doing this labor-and-delivery-with-a-loofah thing, and then the voice-over suggested that singing together might help ease the pain. So the husband began to sing "She'll Be Comin' 'Round the Mountain When She Comes." And the wife seemed to really respond positively. Apparently, nothing gets you through a particularly sharp contraction like Drivin' Six White Horses, or even the mention of Chicken and Dumplings. At least, for some couples.

During our first labor experience, I discovered that rubbing my wife's back and singing "She'll Be Comin' 'Round the Mountain When She Comes" was not as soothing for her as it was for the movie mom. This did not prevent me from trying it on all four of our subsequent births, with essentially the same violent response from my wife.

MISCELLANEOUS TABOOS:

Dads, under no circumstances should you do any of the following:

- Say, "Wow! This takes forever!"
- Text updates to friends and family every fifteen minutes about how this is "taking forever."
- Sing songs about wearing red pajamas, or even whisper, "Oh, we'll all go out to meet her . . ."
- Eat your wife's crushed ice, even though it is so tempting to do so.
- Forget what your baby looks like. Eventually, they'll wheel your baby into a big room full of other babies who look just like yours. Mothers can tell the difference instinctively, but dads, not necessarily. You'll need to memorize which one is yours, or, in some states, you could be charged for negligence.
- Complain about the color of your hospital bracelet.
- Sit in the waiting room and smoke a big cigar, even though, again, it is very, very tempting.
- Make comments about your baby's misshapen head or blotchy skin. Those things are normal for babies. What's your excuse?
- Bring your other children to see the new baby wearing mismatched outfits and messy hair. In this case, your wife will charge you with negligence. This carries far stiffer penalties than those of the state.
- Assume you know how much childbirth hurts. Even if you've passed a kidney stone, so you're pretty sure you know exactly how bad childbirth hurts, you are still not allowed to say so.

And there you have it, fellas! I may not have all the answers, but I'm pretty sure I've made most of the mistakes.

That's gotta count for something.

Regarding the Cliché
Patrick Livingston

Ihate that when you're living your life, and it's your real life—
you're not trying to be funny or quirky or have a special moment—then you sort of jump out of yourself and look around and
think, "This is a bad sitcom! If I were watching this on television,
I'd change the channel." I find myself feeling this way most often
towards "Raising Baby" programs, and yet my life has become one.

It's just a normal night on the Livingston Sitcom. Not even
normal, but extra dull; we're more PBS-style. We drive home a little
late, so we play Daisy's bedtime music (*a compilation of classical music
I force on the family, because it will make Daisy smart, and don't argue with me
about it, because I can only prove my point if she listens to it every night and
naptime and then we wait 21 years to see if it worked and, anyway, if it doesn't
work then it was because of your lack of commitment to the program*). After a
few minutes, we pull into the garage.

I get Daisy out and put her on the ground (*she's 18 months old, so she stands*) while I grab her be-be and horse, and I notice she's picked something up off the floor of the garage and has popped it into her mouth. I freak out, but it's gone. No one will ever know what it was: a raisin, a mouse eye, a bat fetus. It's gone.

My mom has this story she tells about my oldest brother, and how when he was little she'd boil everything from his bottles to his shoes. I guess they didn't have hand sanitizer back then. She was a nut about it, and sweated over a pot of boiling rubber duckies, knowing she was a good mother.

Then one day, her son walked over to the windowsill, picked up a dead fly, put it in his mouth, and swallowed it. At first my mom was horrified, but then she decided that this would be an experiment—although now that I'm writing this, I'm not sure what the experiment was.

"If he dies, I was right to boil the bottles!"

Of course, then her son would be, you know, dead, and all she would have is a pot full of super clean ducks and the thought, If only I had boiled that fly first.

In any case, I'm sure she monitored him closely. She didn't notice any change at all, and, after hours of observation, she put the pot away and never boiled any non-food item again. (*That brother ended up being the biggest handful of all of us, so don't discount boiling the flies just yet.*)

This story bobs though my mind as Daisy starts throwing up just as we step foot in the kitchen from the garage. She lets it go. I don't know at what age we lose this talent, but there is nothing in the world like a child's ability to project body fluids. It only takes a moment, and then Lindsay, Daisy and I all stand stunned at what has just happened.

Daisy looks at the floor with interest at all the new stuff that had not been there just moments before. She doesn't seem sick or sad or bothered; she's very matter-of-fact about her vomit. Her parents, on the other hand, are not playing it cool. We launch into fast-forward, slippery, get the baby out, find the Formula 409, prat-falling madness usually saved for . . . wait for it . . . a TV sitcom. Because it's the end of the day and our mildly clean house is now the same as the bottom of an outhouse, there is an undercurrent of blame cross-fired between parents.

"What did she eat in the garage?!"

"I don't know! Weren't you watching her?"

"What do you mean? I was on the other side of the car!"

"Well, I was getting all the stuff out of the backseat . . . by myself."

"All you had to do was ask for help. Say, 'I'll watch the baby and make sure she doesn't eat anything that might explode from inside her. Would you be a dove and get the diaper bag?'" Finally, my wife asks, "Do you want to clean up the baby or the floor?"

In my assessment of both, it becomes clear that most of what came out shot past the baby and onto the floor. "I'll clean the baby."

One look at my wife, and I know I made the better choice; she doesn't look happy about her lot, but I have a baby to clean up, so I head upstairs. Sure enough, my job is just a quick diaper and costume change. I do, however, get poop on my shirt in the process, so I'm suffering, too.

I worry about Daisy, but figure that whatever she ate she has now been sent on its way, and she's probably just fine. I go down to get her a nice, big sippy cup of milk—her favorite! Stepping over my wife, who is scrubbing Cinderella-style for dramatic effect, I find Daisy's biggest cup and fill it to the brim. I pop it in my sweet baby's mouth and look down to check on Mom's progress. She's just about done, so we wait another minute so Mom can put Daisy to bed.

What? It's her turn! And I have stuff to watch. When the ladies go up to bed, I snuggle into the couch with my friends Jerry, George, and Elaine.

Not two minutes later, I hear screaming from upstairs—full-blown screaming. Not words, just hysteria in the form of vowels. I bound up the stairs because I am a good father—and because my advanced forensic deduction abilities can tell right away what has happened.

The milk is back. At some point during *Good Night, Moon,* Daisy's face erupted, and Lindsay, in an effort to find containment, traveled from the chair, past the crib, into the hallway, over to the bathroom, into the sink, then—because the sink only provides a ski jump for the mess—she finally makes it to the closed toilet, which she eventually, while holding an exploding toddler, opens just as the geyser subsides.

I deduce all this by the perfect line of puke connecting the locations like dots in a coloring book—dots that look suspiciously like the huge cup of milk I saw just moments ago, only it has tripled in size, like magic.

It turns out there is this old saying: "You can only trick your wife into cleaning up your daughter's vomit once." I'd never heard this old saying; I think it's Dutch in origin, but it's true.

I try anyway and immediately chirp, "I'll clean up the baby!"

I insert a big sigh at the beginning, so she knows that mine was the harder choice, but she's gotten wise to me.

"I'll get the baby," she says. "You get the mess."

In my defense, her mess was only on clean linoleum; this vomit is dangerously perched on top of carpet fibers, where one pressured swipe will push the bile deep into the base of the carpet, never to be fully recovered. And this house is a rental. I offer that as both the problem and the solution. I try bargaining, but it is as if the last twenty minutes of wiping up stomach junk alone in the kitchen has made her a different woman.

"If I had known it would happen again," I plead, "I would have been more helpful with the first mess!"

This somehow fails to win her over. She heads off to clean an already clean baby, and I'm left with instructions as to where the Formula 409 is kept.

So here's the cliché: I am waist deep in Formula 409 suds, carpet, and Daisy puke. While I'm feverishly scrubbing, my mind lifts out of my body a little, and I think, This is ridiculous. This moment is so overdone on TV that it's just not funny.

How does parenting become so cliché? Has every parent just done the same stuff over and over and over? Has every mother of a two-year-old given up bottle-boiling after the dead fly experiment? Has every wife maliciously anticipated that this mess will be easier to clean up than the one that follows? Is there any originality left in parenting?

And then, there it is, the smallest little nugget of wisdom to hold on to while I press vomit deeper into someone else's carpet: this has been done before. This same scene has played out in log cabins and palaces, in covered wagons and airplanes, and in hundreds of thousands of rental properties around the world. And someday it will happen in spaceships, which will, of course, have self-cleaning floors. We'll shoot the filth out to space where it will land on some alien's rental carpet.

For millions of years, it has been mankind's job to clean it up, and now, for the first time, it's mine.

I feel the presence of those who have gone before me. I see all the men and women who have been here so many times that it's made this moment cliché. And then, stepping out from the mist I've created by adding baking soda to my cleaning concoction, those parents of the past arrive in my hallway. Together, we scrub. A filthy woman from 15th century England gives me a toothless smile. We join hands and clean. A man in spats and a tuxedo winks and pushes up his sleeves, going to work side by side with a mountain man in a coonskin cap. A knight in full armor stands and shouts, "Blot! Don't rub! Blot! Don't rub!" And he's right, and we cheer and go back to our mess, armed with method and knowledge.

All these thousands of people crammed into my two-bedroom townhouse make me feel like a father. It's not the feeling you get when you first look at your little girl and know you'll take care of her and protect her and never ever let her go on a date, but rather, it's the feeling that you're no longer the selfish boy you once were. That kid who could stay up till 4:00 in the morning playing Sega and eating frozen burritos is long gone; he's now up till 10:30 (*two hours past bedtime*), shoulder to shoulder with an imaginary dwarf spreading sawdust to soak up his daughter's regurgitated milk.

About this time, it occurs to me that Daisy's problem wasn't the thing from the garage floor. If she's still throwing up, it probably means she's sick, maybe even really sick, and all my helpers from the past nudge me into her nursery. Her mother rocks her with her be-be and horse, and I look at her face, and my heart breaks to know that she's sick and there isn't anything I can do about it.

She looks at me and reaches up and repeats the first word she ever said: "Dad-dee." I take her in my arms, and she nuzzles into my neck, and we stand and sway. And only for a moment does it occur to me how cliché this all is—the overprotective parents with vomit on their knees and poop on their shirts, standing in a dark nursery with soft classical music playing, hoping the illness is nothing, but terrified it is something because they're brand new at this and don't know any better.

I wave the cliché away and take this moment and lock it deep in my heart, where I can keep it safe until she's older, or when I'm at work, or when she's at Girls' Camp, or Grandma's, or in the other room, and I feel the pull to hold my daughter, just like this, just as men and women have been doing for millions of years before Daisy and I ever got started.

And I am so thankful to have added to the cliché.

Birthday Boy

Chris Clark

Everyone has a birthday once a year, and my six-year-old son Hugh is no exception. However, for Hugh, his birthday is not just special; it's a manic twenty-four hours in which all things extraordinary, superlative, and borderline apocalyptic happen in a cycle of enduring and repeating phantasmagoria. He starts planning his birthday 364 days earlier—as soon as the smoke clears from the candles—and he talks about his birthday all day every day for the rest of the year. Even Christmas is spent laying plans for the really big day of the year. The boy has expectations.

It's difficult for my wife and me to plan a party that even comes close to the magic going on in Hugh's imagination. Given the chance, Hugh would hand us a menu of celebration options that would have been called "epic" even before the word was hijacked by extreme skateboarders.

Option A: Hugh is awakened up by a real, live SpongeBob SquarePants, who dances around his room throwing candy. Following a breakfast of cotton candy served by circus clowns, Hugh is allowed to ride a pony on the roof (*finally*). Then we go to the Jump on It trampoline emporium and bounce for twelve continuous hours while lunching on Starbursts. The day ends with a community of elves showing up on our front porch bearing cakes made of—you guessed it—more candy.

Option B: The day's events take place inside a laser tag warehouse. There is constant running around and shooting, but instead of shooting lasers, we shoot candy. Hugh wins every time, because everyone else is blindfolded. At a certain point, the laser tag warehouse turns into a giant waterslide, and we swim and slide for hours, with no chance of scraping your back or finding a Band-Aid in the pool at the bottom of the slide. (*We understand that this may be unrealistic.*) The day ends with an Unlimited Friend Sleepover in a house that flies via helium balloons.

Option C: McDonalds is closed to the public for eight hours so Hugh can be fed chicken nuggets intravenously while tramping up and down in the Play Place all by himself. He's allowed to wear shoes in there, no matter what. Then secret agents in dark glasses take Hugh to an underground government lair, where he rides a triceratops. At some point in the day, the entire universe turns into Legos.

Right now, we're looking at Option D: We tell Hugh that once you turn seven, Martians celebrate your birthday for you, freeing you up to do chores and homework, which—as luck would have it—seven-year-olds love to do.

Maybe he'll buy it if we throw in a few Skittles.

The Birds, the Bees, and the Guinea Pigs

Ken Craig

I don't maintain a bucket list, but if I did, "Own a Guinea Pig" would not make the cut, and "Breed Guinea Pigs" would be on a different list, altogether, like the "I Would Sooner Kick the Bucket than Do This" list. But in some of life's great lessons, your life happens to be the punch-line. Nowhere is this truer than in parenting.

Before you and your spouse ever ring that bell that can't be un-rung, round that corner that can't be un-rounded, or empty that toothpaste tube that can't be . . . er . . . you know . . . stuffed back up the tube, nobody can completely, comprehensively explain to you that your post-children brain will never be the same as the pre-children one. Or, how you'll be too tired or too in love to really even care.

In populating the planet—producing replicants who will do unspeakable things to your shirt while you lovingly swaddle them as infants, who will get caught doing impressions of you for their friends during the adolescent years, and who will ignore your savvy, unsolicited advice as young adults – your addled brain will see them as delightful children who won your heart from their very first breath.

There was a time when I would have openly mocked any parent who suggested to my face that I would alter my lifestyle in any way to accommodate children. "Watch Sleeping Beauty at my daughter's request when there's a Seinfeld rerun on? Oh, no," I would retort, putting a brick in my glove and smacking the smugness off their face. "I demand satisfaction. I will not be changing the selfish standard of living I have established."

And then it happened: I had kids. And I morphed into some kind of reputable, lovesick idiot. I suppose I owe an apology to all those soothsayer-parents who foretold my behavior. But it's unlikely they'll get one.

I now live an existence rich with events and acts that were once inconceivable. Have you ever been miles from the nearest rest-stop, squatting outside your minivan in the rain, holding your four-year-old in the air by the sides of his bum so he can "unburden" himself outside the vehicle, to the delight of passing semi-trucks? Ever had your child inform your ecclesiastical leader, "It's a good thing you stopped by our home right now. Usually after 9 p.m. my dad just walks around in his underwear"? In the name of heaven, have you ever looked into your child's eyes and seen the horror in their soul as they realize they're going to be in trouble for taking more than they could eat, so to save them, you finish their bowl of wet, soggy Lucky Charms?

The humanity!

But I do it all. For the love of my brood, I perform acts of service I simply never expect non-parents to understand.

Case in point: Recently, my daughter Abbie decided that her guinea pig, TJ, should have babies. You know, to pass on the TJ family name. To grow her posterity. To leave a legacy during her lifetime.

I didn't have any proof, but my impression was that TJ was probably more interested in having babies because she was going to need someone to take care of her in her old age. Last I checked she had invested virtually nothing in a 401K or IRA account. Most of her life had been spent working part-time gigs as a cage fighter and getting paid under the table, so she wouldn't qualify for Social Security, either. Essentially, her children would be her retirement fund, and if she didn't get busy, she'd end up childless and in a guinea pig homeless shelter.

Abbie assured me we wouldn't have to keep all the guinea pig babies, so I relented and agreed to betroth TJ to the most qualified male guinea pig in the neighborhood. Abbie had recently been to the birthday party of a friend who received, as one of her presents, a male guinea pig. Coincidence? I think not.

So in one of the more awkward phone conversations since "Watson, come here. I need you," we invited this family over one Saturday night and requested they bring their guinea pig Chuck to "meet" TJ. It was all under the guise of Enjoying Dessert Together, but essentially, it was so our guinea pigs could get to "know" each other, to coin a biblical phrase. I don't care where you're from; that's weird.

On top of the weirdness was a generous helping of new emotions on my part. I was suddenly suspicious of Chuck. What kind of guinea pig was he? What was his upbringing? What kind of

27

education did he have? How was he going to provide for this new family of his? If he was like the other guinea pigs I'd met, I could tell you how he was going to provide for them—he wasn't! And then I'd have all these little fatherless guinea pigs running around! Illegitimate guinea pigs, that's what I'd have!

In the end, however, I didn't have the heart to intervene. Who was I to step between two rodents in love? Plus, you should have seen TJ getting ready for her date—checking herself in the mirror every five minutes, on the phone with her girlfriends all day, writing in her diary about how this was the night she was going to give herself to a complete stranger named Chuck.

Chuck showed up fashionably late, and you should have seen the look on his face. It turned out TJ was three times the size of Chuck, outweighing him by at least two pounds. It was a Jack Sprat situation if I'd ever seen one. Then Chuck had the audacity to look at me as if I were to blame. As if to say, "Hey, man, this isn't the order I placed in my mail-order bride catalogue. I ordered Angelina Jolie, not Queen Latifah."

Assuming that guinea pigs are different from humans (*but similar to teenagers*), we stuck these two random guinea pigs in our backyard and fully expected them to mate. Surely the difficult part of this scenario was over. We had a female and a male guinea pig. Now we would just sit back and wait for babies. It was pretty unfair for us to ignore the social pressure we put on these two.

Katie, my wife, put together a delectable salad for TJ and Chuck to enjoy while they got to know each other. You know, to help with the small talk. The evening progressed as the two sat in a grassy spot in the backyard, enjoying their salad and chitchat, all the while trying to ignore the kid paparazzi watching their every move. Sensing that neither TJ nor Chuck was comfortable in the role as exhibitionist, we had the kids come inside the house, and we all enjoyed dessert.

Thirty minutes later, our friends headed to the backyard to retrieve Chuck, and they found him snuggled up next to TJ. Did it take? Did they even try? Had anyone bothered to explain to them how it works? Were they feeling shy? Were they just too full of salad?

The gestational period for a guinea pig is 70 days . . . but I couldn't wait that long to find out. I'd probably sneak into TJ's room when she was asleep and take a peek at her diary to see if we can expect a whole bunch of little TJs in two months. And then I'd explain to Abbie that of course, we love the entire litter and will raise them as our own. Or auction them off at the ward party, which was how TJ came to our home to begin with.

I realize that despite my strict orders for my children to remain the ages they are now, they are, in fact, going to mature. Or at least get older. Sometimes, in the quiet of a late evening, I feel this foreboding awareness that the sacrifices I'll be required to make during the adolescent years will trump anything I've offered up thus far. As a father of a younger brood (*ages two to twelve*), perhaps I'll actually look back longingly at the moments my sacrifices and service merely required holding a child midair as he pooped on my shoes, or venturing into the world of guinea pig mating rituals.

It's possible that parents of teenagers, who have spent a great deal of time and energy insisting that I don't understand the emotional endurance I will be required to demonstrate in the face of eye-rolling, independence-flexing, car-driving, hormonal adolescents might be on to something. And then, because all things come full circle, those parents will be expecting a well-deserved "I'm sorry" from me. This time, however, rather than mock them for suggesting I change my egocentric lifestyle for my children, I'll most likely be humble enough to offer the apology.

Or another brick to the face.

An Epistle to the Roamin'(*s*)

DeNae Handy

A letter written to my children at a time when I was supposed to be preparing an Institute class on Paul's Epistle to the Romans, but found that I could not keep my eyes open, owing to the events of the previous evening, alluded to in the following verses:

Beloved, blessed to be called children by the grace of God and our desire to never have more than twenty dollars at any one time ever again,

Greetings and salutations, from thy mother, bleary-eyed and not very amused to be awakened at this most ungodly of hours.

For doth not the clock read twelve-forty-three? Yea, it doth.

And didst I not dispatch thee to thy beds a mere two hours ago? Yea, I didst.

Wherefore, then, dost thou see fit to roam the halls of our house? Wherefore didst thou shake my shoulder, whispering "Mom, mom," in such manner as to merit thy mother's grumpiest of faces?

Thou saidst to me, "Jake barf-ed. All over."

And I search-ed the heavens for a sign that this wast naught but a vision, albeit a really cruddy one.

But, woe is me, most wretched of mothers!

For 'tis not a vision, nor a dream, nor even the workings of a mind plagu-ed by the consumption of chips and salsa after the hour of the fourth watch, which being interpreted means, 'bout nine-thirty.

Nay, but it is true. Thy brother hath indeed barf-ed.

Fetch him hither, and gettest thou a bunch of towels.

And stoppest thy gagging already. 'Tis thine own fault that thou and thy brother and thy sister have all forsaken thy personal bedrooms in favor of sleeping on the floor as though thou wert puppies or perhaps hobos,

For have I not said, yea, umpteen times, "Gettest thou thy room clean, yea, clearest all this garbage from off thy bed, and sleepest thou therein, like normal people do."

And hast thou not ignor-ed my counsel? Behold, I say unto you, yea, thou hast ignor-ed it like crazy.

Therefore, it is thine own fault that the aforementioned barf hath grac-ed thine own pillow. Copest thou with it, and fetch me now thy brother.

Now, my son, wherefore hast thou dealt thusly with me? Yea, wherefore hast thou barf-ed all over thy sister's white carpet, and thy other sister's pillow, and thy first sister's copy of "Fox Trot?"

Art thou blind? Knowest thou not the path to the potty?

And whilst we art on the subject, what is the cause of this thy barfing? Hast thou contracted the flu? Perhaps the pox of chickens? Hast thou begun chewing tobacco?

Nay, I perceive that it is none of these things. Thou hast barfed because thou wast a glutton at dinner.

Verily, I perceive, both by the workings of my olfactory glands and the vision of noodles amidst the barfage, that thou didst eat ramen and grape soda in porcine quantities, meaning thou wast a total pig.

Yea, I am persuaded that thou didst hog the grape soda for thyself. Didst thou leave any for the rest of us, hmm? Behold, I say unto you, nay.

Furthermore, I now see that there wast also much consumption of Doritos, yea verily, thou didst pretty much put away the whole bag.

Wicked, wicked son! Have I not said from the beginning that thy mother dost not travel the long road to Costco, facing the perils and travails of shopping in such a loony place, just so that thou canst consume every item purchased—including the jumbo packages of butter—within the first six hours of her returning home?

Yea. I have said all of those things. Frequently.

And now, my roamin' son, thou hast receiv-ed the wages of thy transgression. Yea, in spades hast thou receivedst them. Thy wages, I mean. Of, thou knowest, thy transgression. Oh, for heaven's sake, just re-readest it already.

Thy mother sorrowest that thy gluttony hath caus-ed thee to upswallow, yea, to spew, yea, to hurl, to vomit, to basically befoul the entire upstairs and seriously frost thy sisters, who seem now unable to refrain from retching despite dire warnings from me, their mother, that if they, too, vomit, I will bring down wrath upon their brows such as to make Sodom and Gomorrah look like a fairly nice place to settle down and raise a family.

33

I'm not kidding.

Therefore, repent, my son. Forsake thy hoggish ways. Yea, let thy belly be fill-ed with saltines and Pepto Bismol, and never more return to the greedy piggishness that hast brought you to this darkened hall at this ridiculous hour.

Yea, remember, remember my son, that moderation is a virtue, that a little goeth a long way when it cometh to Doritos, and that ramen doeth gruesome things to vacuum cleaners.

And above all, my beloved children, remember,

That grape soda wast for all of us.

Target Practice

Debbie Frampton

My husband has two modes: his What Do We Need to Get Done? mode, and his Motivational Speaker mode. He's one of those who subscribes to the notion that if you tell yourself you love something often enough, eventually it will become true. Apparently it works, because we've been married for 20 years.

To help convince himself and others that they can love hard things, he obtained an I Love It! coin from the Mental Diet Lucky Coin Collection, which is designed to help you focus on a message, idea, or principle that will make your life significantly better. Whenever our kids find themselves facing extreme opposition, he takes out his coin, gets right up in their faces, and shouts, "I love it!"

He keeps shouting until they either jump on the bus, or until I point to his van down by the river and say, "Bu-bye now!"

His coin is not necessarily a bad thing; it has helped me to love Tater Tot casserole, scrubbing toilets, and letting my in-laws live with us for 42 days a year. But I confess that there are times when I want to shove that coin up his nose—usually after I've expressed my unquenchable desire to quit teaching so I can pursue the Holy Grail of writing. Unfortunately, I'm not a fighter, so usually I just put up my white flag and retreat to the bathroom with a box of Girl Scout cookies and a wad of Kleenex.

My daughter is the fighter. She suffered the most gorgeous loss in a split set tie-breaker at her last tennis match of the season. The match went so long that by the time she was halfway through the second set, all the other matches had ended and her teammates had gathered behind the screened fence to watch. You could barely make them out, but you could hear them encouraging her to hang tough. "Come on! Don't give up! You got this!"

I've been to places where this is considered 'illegal coaching', but in Hawaii, it was considered support—to have people on the other side of the fence, cheering you on when you wanted to give up.

In the sports arena, support is pretty cut and dried—a fan paints his face like a bull's eye, waves a pom pom, or yells at the ref—but in the real world, when I paint a bull's eye on my face, my kids throw darts at me. One man's support is another man's target.

Home lunch, for example. Once I nominated myself for Mom of the Year because I woke up early to pack a lunch for my twins' fourth-grade field trip. A home lunch made from scratch. Made with love. Made with my own two hands. Musubi, freshly baked banana muffins, little baggies of Goldfish and apple slices, and to top it off, I poured lemonade into a couple of old Propel bottles and placed them in the freezer to get slushy. I went off to work with visions of my twins dancing in my head—busting into Nacho Libre leaps upon opening their lunches.

"Our life is goooooood," I pictured them saying in a Spanish accent.

In actuality, that's not what they were saying at all. They were saying, "It sucks to be us right now," because apparently every single fourth grader in the school had a better home lunch. Except Haley. Thank goodness Haley only brought a sandwich.

"You only packed us one musubi and everyone else had two!" said twin number one.

"Plus everyone else had Bongos and root beer and Oreos!" said twin number two.

"I feel you!" said my daughter, as if they were sharing a kumbaya. "Mom's sack lunches are just embarrassing."

Say support is like an onion—made up of many layers, or say it's like a box of chocolates—you never know what you're going to get, or say it's like love—with five primary languages. But platitudes are small comfort when you've got a bunch of darts stuck in your face. Support is in the eye of the beholder, or should I say the bull's eye of the beholder. You can feed and clothe your kids and provide a safe, warm place for them to hang loose. You can drive them to every practice and show up at every game. You can buy them a hundred books or a thousand Yugio cards or a million pogs, but don't miss a last minute, optional, lunch-on-the-lawn at the elementary school, or your son may come home with a scowl as deep as the Mariana Trench carved into his forehead.

Then he'll offer up those famous last words: "You never support me!"

And he's not my only child to say those words.

"I know exactly how you feel," said my middle son. "Once I wrote a poem for Mom at school. Everyone in the class got to read theirs to their moms except me, because Mom. Wasn't. There."

"Mom wasn't there for my 6th grade graduation either," added my daughter.

Ummm . . . I was kinda out of the country.

It mattereth not how many things you do right; the things that stick to memory are the things you do wrong. Not to mention the things you say wrong. I usually try to say as little as possible, choosing neutral phrases that connote compassion and can't be misconstrued as negative.

For instance, after my daughter lost her tennis match, we went to Costco and ordered pizza. She said, "I'm tired."

And I said, "I bet."

"I knew you were going to say 'I bet'!" she said. "You always say 'I bet' after I say I'm tired. I don't know why I bother telling you I'm tired, because I already know you're going to say 'I bet.'"

Is there something more appropriate I should be saying? Like I'm tired too, so quit your whining? "I bet" just sums it up so succinctly. It's much more pointed than saying, Of course you're tired—it's inevitable after playing varsity tennis while simultaneously playing on two select soccer teams and qualifying for the National History Day competition. You deserve the world's longest nap, girlfriend.

Then my daughter rubbed her temples and said, "I have a headache."

"I bet!" I said, only this time, verbally bolding, capitalizing and punctuating it to encapsulate what I really meant to say, which was of course, After a match like that, you deserve to have the world's largest headache.

She rolled her eyes and said, "Mom, you have pizza in your teeth."

I should have elaborated. I should have said, Of course I have pizza in my teeth! That's like saying I have fillings in my teeth. I'm old, I have children, and I eat at Costco.

But I didn't. Just as I wouldn't have elaborated if my middle son had said, I need a massage, or if my twins had said, we want to raise roosters, or if my husband had said, I feel like giving a motivational speech right now. I simply took another bite of pizza and said, "I bet!"

I think being a mom loosens your grip on reality somehow. Not all at once, but gradually, like a slow gas leak—undetected until one morning you wake up in a coma, and you think, When did I slip into this coma?

When you first have kids, you're still cool. You're still down with it. But then one day, you get pulled up on stage during an elementary school assembly because the PTA president needs a few moms to dance in one of the numbers. I was a cheerleader in the 80s for goodness' sake, so I'm always up for that sort of exhibitionism. I can Flashdance, I can Moonwalk, I can Back the Bus Up, baby. If you need a Roger Rabbit or a Running Man, I'm your mom! I got up on that stage and rocked the house.

"That's my mom doing the worm!" I imagined my boys nudging the kid next to them. "Bet you've never seen a Superbowl Shuffle like that!"

But as I was doing The Sprinkler, I made eye contact with one of the kids in the crowd and recognized the deer-in-the-headlights expression on his face and the big L on his forehead. It was my son, and instantly I was one of those moms. One of the moms who thinks she's got all right moves, but they're in all the wrong places.

The transition to being one of those moms isn't easy. It takes time to come to terms with the possibility that you might not be meeting your children's expectations or needs in real life as well as you are in your imagination. It takes even longer to figure out that maybe these children are God's way of saying, "Open wide. Here comes a taste of your own medicine!"

I'm not above saying I probably deserve it, since I often accuse my husband of being unsupportive, usually after I announce that I'm going to quit working and cleaning and letting his parents live with us for 42 days a year so I can write funny stories full time. Poor guy is like a walking target, bless his heart. It's just too bad my primary love language isn't that's-just-not-practical, or okay-but-we'll-have-to-tighten-our-belts.

Once in a while, however, he really hits the mark. Like at our last visit to the dentist. He got the chatty hygienist—the one who breaks out flow-charts, flip-boards and Power Points to teach us that our middle finger, not our index finger, is most effective when flossing. The chatty hygienist's room is wall-to-wall cat collages, and once the cleaning commences, so do the cat stories.

On one particular visit, she had to interrupt my cleaning to blow her nose after telling me about the time her cat was in a coma for three months. Her cruel and unusual husband kept insisting that it was time to pull the plug, but she could feel the cat wasn't ready. Had it not been for the wedge jacking up my mouth, I may have shared with her that flossing isn't the only occasion where the middle finger is most effective.

After my husband's cleaning, he cornered me in the waiting room.

"Pssst, come 'ere," he whispered, his eyes as big as quarters. "There's something you have to see." And then he led me back to the chatty hygienist's room. "She just got back from Taiwan," he told me with a grin, motioning to several 8x10 photos pinned up on the wall among the cat collage. There she was holding a cocktail and lounging with a couple of tigers at a monastery. And there she was setting a pick on a couple of orangutans in yellow basketball shorts. And there she was waving to the camera as if she had no idea there was a gigantic albino boa constrictor hanging from her neck.

"Look at this one," my husband said, pointing to a photo of an elephant with a paintbrush perched in his trunk. "She adopted an elephant." He paused for effect. "First she had to catch the elephant, and then she had to wash him and ride him through the jungle for ten days." Next to the photo was an impressionist painting of a bouquet of flowers. "Not Monet," he whispered. "Her elephant painted it for her."

"She's coo-coo for coconuts," I said under my breath.

"Isn't it great?" my husband said. "I couldn't wait to show you. I thought it would be perfect to add to your collection of funny stories."

To say the cat got my tongue may not be the most appropriate phrase to describe what happened next, but I was dumbstruck. The room fell away, until the only thing in focus was a big-screened fence. My husband stood behind it with a bull's eye painted on his face.

"Come on! Don't give up! You got this!" he shouted.

I took his hand and stammered, "This . . . is the nicest . . . thing . . . you've ever done for me."

He looked puzzled at first, but then a flash of light crossed his face. "You know what I feel like doing right now?" he asked softly.

"What?"

"Giving you a motivational speech."

"I bet," I smiled.

Israelite Girls Camp

DeNae Handy

I'm the woman who sucks all the fun out of the room in those "Getting to Know You" games by sanctimoniously declaring that my favorite book is Isaiah. Until then, all the other players were content to list *Pride and Prejudice* or *Sense and Sensibility* as delightful reads. Then I came along and made everyone else feel like a heretic. One of these days I expect a mob of fed-up Jane Austen lovers to take a chapter out of Acts and stone me.

I can't help it. I love the scriptures. And for the better part of twenty years, I've been a teacher in the LDS Church, one of the great joys of my life.

One year I taught an Old Testament class in Institute, a program which offers college-level religion classes for credit. While

I was slogging through Leviticus—great stuff if you're into the rules and regs of the Mosaic Law, which I am—I came across a verse in chapter 18 that had to do with women and their—ahem—"'lady weeks." Specifically, Moses was instructing the men to stay away from the gals during, you know, that time.

As I considered this particular injunction, it occurred to me that of all the commandments given to those Israelite men, this was probably the easiest one to keep:

Moses: Okay, now that we have the Ten Big Ones out of the way, the next item is food.

Israelites: We're losing our doughnut privileges, aren't we?

Moses (*consulting stone tablet agenda*): Manna. That's it.

Israelites: Can we deep fry that stuff? (*snicker, snicker*)

Moses: Next, we've got stick collecting. Don't do it on the Sabbath. I mean it.

That One Guy Who Always Pipes up in Meetings: What'll happen if we forget?

Moses: I can't emphasize enough the importance of not forgetting. You won't enjoy it.

TOGWAPUIM: Yeah, but...

Moses: Seriously. Shut up.

TOGWAPUIM: I just...

The Israelite sitting next to TOGWAPUIM: Dude, if you forget, God will do to you what I'm gonna do to you if you raise your hand one more time . . .

Moses: Ok, next item: women.

Israelite Men (*sitting up*): That's more like it.

Moses (*clears throat; loosens tie*): When your wives are, you know, having that—er, that week...

TOGWAPUIM: What w—? Ow! Geez! That hurt!

Moses: The Lord wants you to just leave them alone.

(a long, thoughtful silence falls over the congregation)

Israelites: That's it?

Moses: Yep. Don't touch 'em.

(further pondering; the occasional furtive glance; one or two "beats me" shrugs)

Tentative Israelite Spokesman: Um. To clarify: The commandment says "Thou shalt not touch the shrieking, hormonally insane, prickly pear that possesses thy otherwise lovely and reasonable spouse one week a month"?

Moses: Words to that effect, yes.

(understanding slowly dawns)

Israelites: Well, gosh, no sweat! We were practically born to keep that one!

(fist-bumps all around)

So, as I was considering this scene, I imagined what it must have been like to live in those conditions for forty years. Remembering that for one week, women were considered "unclean" (*read: scary and kinda mean*) and were therefore sent outside the main camp to simmer down and write their apology notes, I started running a few numbers. And let me tell you, the math is downright terrifying:

To keep things simple, let's assume there were a million Israelites and that exactly half of them were women. That's 500,000 ladies.

Now, let's assume that half of them were too old, too young, or too pregnant to have one of those weeks. That leaves 250,000 qualifiers. Divide that number by four weeks of the month, and on any given week, you would have *(are you ready for this?)* SIXTY-TWO THOUSAND, FIVE HUNDRED WOMEN ripping their tents apart looking for chocolate and threatening to burn the next pair of socks they find in the middle of the floor when there is a perfectly good hamper right there in plain sight although of course everyone else in this family is obviously blind and why do you all have to *breathe so loud??*

For fun, take it a step further and consider that this also meant 62,500 women in a P-sychotic M-ental S-tate, and another 62,500 laying eggs, and . . . well, let's just say these were dark, frightening times in which to live. A war with the Philistines was a walk in the park by comparison, as it gave the men a chance to get out of the house for a few days.

It could be argued that the wisest thing Moses ever did was send these ladies to "Girls' Camp."

In my home, we have three females of hormonal eligibility. This means the three men in the family have been under siege for years. How nice would it be to announce to your 14 year-old— currently shredding her little brother for sneezing during her nap— that it's time to start packing for camp?

"Leave early," you could suggest. "Pick up Shelby on the way. Her mom says she's been bawling since Wednesday."

You see? This is why I love the scriptures. So many insights and opportunities for self-discovery are contained in the pages of Holy Writ. I'd love to share more with you, but judging by the sounds of overturned furniture coming out of my daughter's bedroom, I need to find a suitcase for my husband.

I just hope the Philistines are in town . . .

Raising Men

Joshua Bingham

Warning: This essay depicts the death and plucking of two chickens. Reader discretion is advised.

When I was a missionary in Italy, there was a member—Ercole—who lived on a farm deep in the Abruzzo, the agricultural heart of Italy. One day he asked my companion and me if we wanted some chicken. I had visions of neatly packaged chicken in a farmhouse freezer. When we arrived to pick it up, he took us out back to a pen full of live, clucking, squawking, pecking chickens.

My companion, who grew up on a farm, walked right into the pen, cornered a chicken, and scooped it up by its feet. I felt satisfied and was ready to head back to our little apartment.

"Aren't there other missionaries in your apartment?" Ercole asked. "You need more than one! Take another!"

I shuffled into the chicken coop, my hair catching on the wire overhead. Certainly I could catch a chicken! My companion had made it look so easy. I took a deep breath and threw myself into the feathered melee. The chickens scattered, and I stumbled around the coop like a fool, snatching ineffectively at the heads of fleeing poultry.

I had never been forced to catch my own food, and I didn't want to embarrass my companion or the generous farmer. I assumed that a chicken felt the same as I would about being scooped up by someone trying to eat me. With each attempt, I hesitated, worried that I'd learn firsthand what it meant to be hen-pecked.

The harder I tried to corner a bird, the more flustered I became. Knowing that I couldn't let this ridiculous performance continue much longer, I focused on one chicken that looked slightly tastier than the rest, and I did what any man in my situation would do.

I slapped it.

Everyone—including my dinner—looked stunned at my choice of offensive tactics. I made a grab for the inert chicken's ankles and, carefully stepping over the day's survivors, I hoisted my prize over my head. I emerged from the coop victorious.

Ercole took both of the chickens from us, and in a swift, professional manner, snapped their necks and put them in an apple crate. I stood there aghast. I'd never seen death dispatched so quickly and efficiently. But neither he nor my companion seemed to give the birds' execution a second thought, so I tried to play it cool.

We piled into the back of Ercole's tiny Fiat Cinquecento—me, my companion, and a box with two dead chickens in it—and headed back to our apartment in the city.

When we got home, I was at a complete loss as to what to do with those two dead birds. Again, my companion's farm upbringing came in handy. He put a large pot of water to boil and showed me how to scald and pluck the birds. It was horrible and strangely satisfying all at once, kind of like popping bubble wrap in reverse. If you scalded the bird correctly, the feathers came off in handfuls. I remember seeing bits of white fluff float from our balcony, drifting on the open air. I worried that the old woman living below us would complain. After all, she got angry when rainwater dripped from our balcony to hers.

When it came time to gut the chickens, I was out; I just didn't have the stomach for it. My companion again took the lead. Soon there were two mostly-plucked chickens roasting in our oven. Bits of feather blackened on their ankles where it had been too hard to pluck.

I didn't eat chicken that night. After the catching, killing, plucking and gutting, I felt I had had enough chicken for the day.

I'm grateful to live in a post-industrial society where I don't have to kill my meals. Perhaps I'm not as manly as the generations who preceded me; I certainly don't have the chops to kill and butcher my own meat. The whole experience made me uncomfortable and squeamish, and the smell nearly put me off chicken entirely. Thankfully, I live in a world where the definition of manhood is changing and evolving.

My grandpa was a cowboy. I don't know if he rode the open range exactly, but he did own a dairy farm and kept a stable full of draft horses. During the summer, we helped bale hay from his fields to provide feed for the cattle during the winter. I think Grandpa could do almost anything—birth a cow, fix a fence, build a barn, drive a tractor. It was all in a day's work. An old shed behind his house was full of all sorts of tools we kids marveled at. We could only guess at their purpose.

My dad is much the same way. He's not officially a cowboy,

though judging by the amount of cowboy poetry we listened to as kids, you'd think otherwise. Even though he's an engineer, he's truly his father's son. He works hard at his job—when he finds time between golf games—but on weekends, he has been known to build a shed big enough to house a small family, or run a sprinkler system in my brother's yard, or rewire the entire electrical system in the basement of my house.

When my wife and I had our first baby, my father made us a beautiful dresser and bookcase for the nursery. They were nicer than anything you could find at a high-end furniture store.

As kids, we went on the deer hunt every year, and I have distinct memories of the few times we did get a deer. Dad hung it up by a chain in the garage and proceeded to process and butcher the thing until the meat was neatly wrapped in paper in the deep freeze.

The skills possessed by my grandfather and my dad seemed to be real man skills. And as I became a husband and later a father, I wondered how I had missed the "real man skills" class. I could no more butcher a deer than compete in pairs figure skating in the Olympics. Over the years I have learned a few basic home-repair skills, but I don't imagine I'll ever build my own furniture anytime soon. I get bored by sporting events and am by no means an athlete of any kind. (*Assuming competitive Diet Coke drinking doesn't count. Okay. Then, no I'm not an athlete.*)

However, I love to cook. I make a mean lasagna, delicious Monte Cristos and the creamiest crème brûlée you ever tasted. When we buy fresh flowers, I'm the one responsible for arranging them. I frost and trim our kids' birthday cakes. I love design and decorating.

My wife and I have spent many hours arranging and

rearranging stacks of books, ceramic birds and vases on bookcases and shelves around the house until we hit it just right. I write. I blog. I sing in the ward choir.

For those keeping score, none of these are on the dossier for a typical manly man.

My two oldest children are boys, and I feel a sense of obligation to teach them to be men—a thought that's a little terrifying for me sometimes. I feel like I'm still in the process of defining my own manhood. If I could choose, I would almost hope my boys followed the more typical path of playing sports, camping, scouting and other manly pursuits. In many ways it might make their lives smoother and easier.

But I can't teach them how to do those things. Hopefully I can help them see a few truths I have learned as I have sought to define my own manhood.

Although I can't offer batting or catching tips at baseball practice, I can be at every game and cheer my son on—even if I'm reading my Kindle between innings. A real man supports his kids, in whatever they do.

When I was a senior in high school, I had the lead in the musical. Since my dad isn't really up to speed on the musical theatre canon, he never connected my character's name with the star of the show. My sister told me about sitting in the auditorium, perusing the program and waiting for the show to start, when suddenly, Dad noticed that I had top billing.

Panicked, he turned to my brothers and sisters. "Wait! Josh has the lead! Does anyone know if he can sing?!" When I came on stage at the curtain call, to take my bow, there was Dad in the audience, crying. I knew then that he loved me and believed in me, even if the way I chose to spend my free time was completely foreign to him.

I may not be able to teach my kids how to repair a squeaky door or build a bookcase. But I will teach them the truth that all real men should know: the workers at Home Depot can pretty much walk you through how to do anything. And a real man isn't afraid to ask for help.

True, I'll probably never kill my own pig and turn him into artisanal sausages. But if someone else will handle the slaughtering, I can turn that sausage into a mean Tuscan soup with white beans and kale. I'll even bake the bread to serve on the side. Because a real man knows how to accept his limitations, and how to adapt.

And even though I've forsaken the fall deer hunt in favor of the fall TV season launch, I have finally become comfortable in my manhood. I will never be that guy who throws a game-winning pass, who changes the oil in his own car, or puts up a barbed-wire fence around the north forty. I hope more than anything that I can teach my sons to be proud of who they are, and how to be comfortable in their own skin, regardless of what the world tells them is normal or typical. Because that, in my mind, is truly being a man.

Gettin' the Heck Outta Dodge

Ken Craig

I have never felt defined by the car I drive. My dad cured me of this when, on my 16th birthday, he gave me a 1976 Honda Civic that had been sitting idle in the garage since 1952. The original paint had faded (*I'm assuming, since no self-respecting car should ever be this shade of orange*), there was no air conditioning, no stereo, and the passenger seat was broken, so that the left half of the seat kind of fell to the side, letting the passenger rest on the driver's shoulder. This was perfect for dates, but not so great for Steve, my friend and customary passenger.

Anyway, being 16, I threw in a stereo and the car was perfect. I couldn't care less about what anybody else was driving, or how I looked cruising through the high school parking lot listening to Beastie Boys with Steve nestled on my shoulder. In fact, I specifically remember one time seeing a guy get out of his Chevy Camaro in the parking lot, and blasting from his car stereo for all the high school to hear, was Lionel Richie's "Dancing on the Ceiling." I thought to myself, "How embarrassing for him. Truly, he's (*Nerdy*) Like Sunday Morning." So clearly, to me, music was more defining of somebody's character than the car he drove.

And now, as an adult, I am equally disinterested in the car model I own. My criterion is that the vehicle be able to comfortably get me from one place to another as inexpensively as possible. Alas, one recent summer, our Dodge Caravan no longer performed this basic task, so I finally had to drive it out into the desert and shoot it.

We bought the van when it had about 42,000 miles on it. At the time of death, it had logged 193,842. It had wanted to die months earlier, but our family just wouldn't let it.

The final hoorah for this poor van was a trip from Las Vegas, Nevada to Breckenridge, Colorado for a family reunion vacation.

We left Vegas and headed north that fateful August morning. The Vegas sun was up so it was already 146 degrees. We got about three hours into the trip, just outside of Cedar City, Utah, when the air conditioning went out. It wasn't Las Vegas Hot, but it was still miserable. Hours later we were all sweaty, stinky, suffering from heat exhaustion and a little bit cranky. The stereo had gone out on the van several months prior to this trip – rendering the car useless for quite some time already – so we just drove in silence. Nobody was saying much to anybody, unless they were breathing threatening remarks about staying on their side of the seat or making eye contact for too long.

As we finally reached Breckenridge, the temperatures were bearable; however, this was the same time that the transmission decided to hiccup. Nothing dramatic, but it gave me pause for all of three seconds until I was immediately distracted by the fun and frivolity of family and outdoor recreation, wrapped up in a delightful climate. No sense worrying about the van. Who knows if we'll ever really need it again?

The fun ended and all distractions ceased as five days later we prepared to journey back home. Coming out of Breckenridge, we stopped at a gas station, and, sensing more hiccups, I poured some transmission fluid into the van. Truth be known, I resented even spending that much money on this limping vehicle. I didn't want to put one more dime into this sucker. Not for the transmission, not for the air conditioning, not 25¢ to pump up the tire. Nothing. All I needed was to push this baby another 10 hours, and then she could give up. I wanted her to coast right into our driveway and pass away, the way Johnny Depp's boat sank just as he stepped onto the pier.

I stood outside the van in that gas station parking lot, visually and emotionally taking in the risk directly in front of me. The air was still; the family already sweating. But I knew we could make it. We had to make it!

I made direct eye contact with the sun. He stared right back at me, unflinching. A particularly round tumbleweed blew by, past the gas pump, off into the vacant landscape. Somewhere in the distance, a dog barked. All life's trials had let me to this point.

I looked into the van and locked eyes with Katie. She pulled her sunglasses to the tip of her nose, stared back at me...and then with all the unspoken understanding of a couple married 16 years, she winked. She had my back.

I slid into the driver seat.

"Belts," I ordered.

"Locked," the kids responded in well-trained unison, like the command unit they are.

"Snacks," I gave the next order.

"Loaded," they responded.

"People, we're gonna hit this road hard, and we're gonna hit it fast." (*Pause for dramatic effect as I turn the key and give this pitiful beast of a vehicle a push on the gas.*) "Let's do this!"

Three hours later, my pep talk was losing its shine, but I was still feeling pretty confident. The transmission seemed to be holding up and we were making good time. But then, somewhere in the vast wasteland that is western Colorado/eastern Utah, my three-year old daughter, Roxanna, started to complain about feeling nauseous.

"My tummy hurts!" she said.

"It's the heat, Sweetie," said Katie. "Have a drink of water."

"But it really hurts!" said Roxanna.

"Just hang on," said Katie.

"Baaaaaarrfffffff!" said Roxanna.

This was no ordinary barf. This was a barf of epic proportions. This was the barf all other barfs hope to be when they grow up. To make matters worse, Roxanna had eaten an obscene amount of pizza before we left. To make matters even *more* worse, my oldest daughter was sitting in front of Roxanna, directly in the line of fire. To make matters the *most* worse, it was 112 degrees, so we now had Barf Potpourri permeating the car for everyone to enjoy.

Katie climbed to the back of the van, holding out a towel for Roxanna to barf into for what seemed like longer than your average span of Child Vomit Time. There was nothing but freeway around.

No towns, no rest stops, no gas stations, no off ramps…nothing. So I kept barreling down the highway in search of a service station, or, barring that, a cliff.

"I told you my tummy was hurting!" Roxanna said.

"WWWAAAAAAAAAAAHHHHHHH!" said my 20-month old, Tanner, who was sick to death of his car seat and was just happy to join in the anarchy.

"JUST WATCH YOUR DVD!" I suggested calmly to any children who weren't yakking up pizza.

"I can't SEE the DVD! I have pizza barf in my hair!" screamed Abbie. "This is the worst birthday ever!"

Finally, I saw a Shell gas station and convenience store. Out in the middle of nowhere, with no neighboring town, there was a Shell station. I didn't know where the employees were bused in from, and frankly, I didn't care.

I pulled off the freeway, behind this 18 Wheeler. But before the off ramp ended, the truck lost a gi-normous tire, and I hit it. I mean, I hit it hard. The entire planet turned suddenly silent and, in slow motion and with just as much gravity, we clocked in the same air time as the Apollo 13's flight around the moon. Houston…we definitely have a problem.

And as we limped into the gas station, I could hear something underneath the van, dragging on the ground.

I got out to take a look. And there was this thing hanging from the van. There were no fumes, no leaks or drips – just a dangly thing where no dangly thing should be. So, being the mechanic that I was, I knew exactly what do to.

"Where is your duct tape?" I asked the attendant.

"Over there," she half-pointed, putting out her cigar.

"And your Wet Wipes?"

"We don't have any."

I couldn't have heard her correctly.

"I'm sorry? You don't have any what, exactly?"

"Wet wipes. We're out."

"You're out? Of wet wipes? Define 'out,' please." I was driving a Roman vomitorium. I needed some hope to cling to. "How 'out'? Like, in the storage room 'out,' or…"

Slowly, silently, she looked up at me from her Hunting magazine. Startled, I shuffled two feet back from her, knocking into a Hostess stand and bumping a rack of cupcakes onto the floor. I found myself unable to make eye contact with her, convinced she would stab me with the bathroom key if I didn't beat it.

Hoping that some sort of Three Nephites intervention would save my life, I grabbed my duct tape and a bunch of ice cream bars for my desolate family, and then bolted for the parking lot with faith that I would see sunlight again and my death would not become some weird cautionary tale for Boy Scouts about how they should always be prepared and at least know the basics about car maintenance.

While Katie secured her place in Heaven by cleaning up the barf and the people covered in it, I channeled my inner-caveman and duct-taped the pipe hanging from the bottom of the van. All tidy and secure, we were on our way. We still had hours to go, and though there were moments of uncertainty with the transmission, the heat, the jerry-rigged pipe under the van and the likelihood of my losing the one final marble rolling around in my head, by the grace of Dodge manufacturing and the longest prayer I've ever offered, we somehow made it safely into our driveway.

Once I hoisted every last body out of the van and into their bed, I went back outside and made my peace with that ol' Dodge. Her time had come. The next day, we gave her to a mechanic-friend of ours to fix up and sell for whatever he could get. I find myself hopeful that she's still around town somewhere, doing some good for somebody else. Our time with her is over now, but she'll always have our love ... our love ... our Endless Love.

I Do, Already

DeNae Handy

In case there was any doubt before, it's official: my husband and I are thoroughly married. All those years together—the kids, the bills, the arguments over whose feet are coldest—were mere hints. On a recent Tuesday afternoon, our union was consummated in what can only be described as an act of sublime intimacy.

It took place in a parking lot, with a fairly sizable matinee audience. That's how we roll in Vegas, baby.

One of the benefits of finally having all of the kids in school is being able to meet my husband for lunch at least once a week. By my calculations, it's seven thousand times better than going out together at night.

For starters, we're both awake, already a significant distinction from most Friday evenings. Since we're usually coming from work or class, we're dressed nicely; one of us is even wearing makeup. And anyone in the vicinity under the age of 25 is only there to bring us food and keep a head on the Diet Coke.

I'm thinking of starting a religion where this is the definition of heaven.

This particular Tuesday, after a delightful meal spent finishing sentences and planning family vacations without some teenager Facebooking the whole discussion in a status play-by-play—

"We're going to San Diego in August!"

"Wait, now we're just going to Mesquite."

"Never mind. We're staying home and cleaning the garage."

"I hate family vacations."

—we were standing next to my car, saying our dewy farewells.

Me: What time do you think you'll be home tonight?

Him: Depends. When does your last piano student leave?

Me: What does that have to do with anything?

Him: Nothing. I just want to know if I need my white-noise headphones. I left them in my gym bag.

Me: Please, stop. The abundance of support is suffocating.

You know—that kind of flirting.

Then, in a gesture of tender familiarity, my husband looked deep into my eyes, reached his hand up to my cheek—and took hold of a hair growing out of my "beauty mark."

"Ow! Let go!" I yelped. "It's attached!"

"I know. It's long enough to be attached to your scalp." And he gave the hair a yank.

"Did you get it?" I asked, rubbing my cheek.

"Nope. It's really anchored in there."

"Well, here," I said, reaching into my purse. "Use these tweezers."

Remember, we were standing in a restaurant parking lot. On a Tuesday. At lunchtime.

My husband took hold of my chin to get better traction. "Hang on," he said, squinting. "I can't see it clearly. Turn more toward the sunlight."

Obediently, I turned. This was, after all, a rogue hair sticking out of my face. When you get to be my age, you take that sort of thing personally.

This time, he pushed down on my head as though I might otherwise spin away like a top, lined up the tweezers, and yanked again.

"Dang! I think I felt my gums separate."

"Yep. You could tether the Queen Mary with that sucker." He was triumphant. "Look at it!" We both examined the tweezers closely, me in that chin-up/eyes-down position that just screams 'bifocals.'

"Well, at least it's—"

"Just a second, there's another one on your neck."

Traction. Alignment. Yank.

"Okay, thank—"

"Wow. You've got a complete arboretum here on your chin."

Yank, yank, yank.

"All right, I'll take it fr—"

"I don't think I can get them all. They're like Ents. Ha!" Now he was getting clever. "Look out, Orcs! DeNae's chin is gonna knock down your nasty old towers!"

For his money, you just couldn't have enough *Lord of the Rings* references in a given conversation. "Yes, dear, you're terribly witty. Give me the tweezers, please."

"We'll start calling you—"

"Watch it," I said. "Any name ending in '-beard' earns you the privilege of sleeping in your car."

"Sorry," he said, not sorry at all. "At any rate, I don't have time to uproot the whole forest. You'd better wax before we leave on our trip." We were heading to a conference in Orlando, where I was sure that any presentation on the subject of my chin hairs would still have been more interesting than what was on the agenda.

He handed me the tweezers and grinned. "Don't want the other Feds thinking I'm married to a guy."

"No," I said. "We certainly can't have that. I'll take care of it tonight."

He started toward his car.

"Oh, honey?" I called to him. "One more thing."

He turned back.

"Was this as good for you as it was for me?"

He grabbed me roughly around the waist, and kissed me hard. Twenty-five years into this gig, and he can still turn my insides to jelly. "Better," he growled.

I kissed him again. "Glad to hear it," I murmured, straightening his tie, "because there's more where that came from."

He raised an expectant eyebrow.

"You could hide a tribe of Aborigines in the hair growing out of your nose," I breathed into his ear. "We're going to have to take care of that when you get home."

He laughed and winked. "It's a date."

SECTION TWO

"Nearly all the best things that came to me in life have been unexpected, unplanned by me."

Carl Sandburg

Non-Traditional

Becca Wilhite

"Mom!" She hollers as if our house were much bigger than this. "Mom." She slams the door. "Mom." She drops her backpack on the kitchen floor, which is just that much easier than hanging it on a hook designed for that exact purpose.

The angst-ridden preteen sigh comes now, followed by that nearly perfect look of contempt. "We have to write an essay on family traditions."

I can't quite tell if the contempt is directed toward this (obviously) ridiculous assignment or toward me—the only mom in the world who doesn't do anything cool.

But I can guess.

She's right. We don't have traditions. We've done our share of Easter-egg hunting, but always on the coattails of someone else's hard work. We don't have a summer vacation tradition or a first day of school ritual or a special plate to eat from on birthdays. I'm way more likely to grouse about "Satan's Holiday" than do any Halloween decorating.

Thanksgiving is a Grandma holiday, always spent at one in-law home or another. And even Christmas is pretty relaxed (you know, for me).

It's not like I don't know how to do traditions. I recognize them. I've watched my mother-in-law bust out an entirely green dinner for St. Patrick's Day. My parents used to wake us up at some indecent hour to do a "Sunrise Service" for Easter morning. April Fool's Day is actually right up my husband's alley, so we all walk on tiptoes around here on that day, just in case he's in a fooling mood.

I know what it is. I know how to do it. I just . . . don't. I'm too lazy to bring it all about.

The girl still stands, staring just past me with that disgusted look on her sweet face. I grasp. I rack the brain. I open my mouth, and this is what comes out: "Chocolate chip cookies for dinner."

She blinks and focuses on me for just a second. Then she shakes her head, dismissing me and my stupid, Mom-ish ideas.

"Why not? It's something we do, over and over, at a specific time of year. Isn't that what makes a tradition?" Come on, kid. Validate me.

She squints, as if to read my hidden agenda. "Really? You'd let me tell?"

Sweet. Now we're co-conspirators. "Sure. Go for it."

She leaps up on a kitchen stool and starts scribbling on a page of notebook paper. Her left arm covers what she's written, so I can't read it before she's ready to share. But it doesn't really matter; I know what she's going to say.

She's going to tell about how I make chocolate chip cookies for dinner every New Year's Eve, because we'll be snacking on veggie trays, and some delicious cold ham, and expensive cheese and high-quality bread all night long.

She's going to tell how I grin and whisper, "Don't tell anyone that this is your dinner." And how everyone laughs and nods and double-pinky-promises to never, ever tell.

But when I swipe her arm away, I see the phrase "roll over in her grave" on the page. What? Wait. What?

I yank the paper off the counter and read about how this poor kid's mom only does one tradition, and it would horrify her own mother, may she rest in peace, if she even thought the grandchildren were being fed white flour and butter-based foodstuffs as a main meal.

I can't even argue. Bummer. I slide to the floor in defeat and pass back her paper. Then the plotting starts. Maybe I could invent a tradition on the spot, and she could write about that. Maybe something involving some obscure holiday that gets sadly overlooked. Arbor Day, maybe. Or Gunpowder Day (November 5th, and feel free to look it up if you don't believe me).

After the pathetic attempt at inventing a family tradition, I get defensive. Who has time for that sort of frivolity, anyway? There's too much going on. What kind of mother spends hours and hours doing the exact same thing over and over? Sounds like a distinct lack of imagination to me.

Grumble, grumble. Darn those clever mothers, with their foresight and their artistic ideas and their follow-through. And their energy. I barely have energy to get dinner on the table every night.

What? Wait. What? Every night? Over and over? The same thing, at the same time? Realization settles on my shoulders like a hot towel out of the dryer. I have a tradition. We have a family tradition.

We eat dinner together every night.

We eat.

Dinner.

Together. Every night.

And we have done it for years. All the years of my kids' lives.

Granted, it was easier when the kids were small. Nobody expected them to leave the house in the evening. Nobody else wanted them at the witching hour. They were always home. When sports and activities and jobs started encroaching on our dinner time, I got a little Mama Bear about it. I swiped those invaders away with my paw for as long as I could. Gradually I realized that I had to be willing to give a little. And you know what? I still resent it. I resent anything, any scheduling conflict that gets in the way of my dinner with my family.

Life with older kids means we have new and uglier schedules. People expect something of us. Don't they know that they can expect all they want, but not at the cost of our family dinner? I grumble about it. But I have to roll with it, at least some of the time. The dinner still happens, even if not everyone is there. And there's a hole. An empty chair at the table is a hole in my heart.

Because it's our tradition. We love food. We love bread food and salad food and meat food and cheesy food. We love watermelon, and twice-baked potatoes. We love smoothies and sandwiches and pasta and soup. We love the homemade.

We love the hanging around together. We love the laughing and even the complaining. We love the connection. We love it when a friend shows up at the door, or stays into the dinner hour, and we have to bring the piano bench into the kitchen so everyone can have a seat at the table.

We pray together. We talk together. We laugh together. We eat deliciousness. We clean up together. We search out dessert together, too. Sometimes, we even find it.

So if you show up at our door, you're not likely to find clever homemade holiday decorations or any kind of glorious production. But if you're here between 5:00 and 6:30, you can bet on finding us in the kitchen, up to our elbows in something tasty, reveling in our favorite family tradition.

What I Never Knew I Wanted

Stephanie Sorensen

I never made one of those spiral notebooks where you glue in pictures of wedding dresses and swatches of fabric for your future bridesmaids' colors. I don't think I was a particularly morose or lonely child; I just didn't fantasize about marriage and certainly not about motherhood. I had a hard time picturing myself married, and my limited experience with babysitting hadn't unlocked some latent desire to birth and diaper babies. I couldn't picture myself cleaning a house and whistling songs. I couldn't picture myself loving somebody enough to want to be with them more than I wanted to do anything else or be anything else. And I definitely didn't ever picture myself walking down the stairs to find my own children pouring red Gatorade into the off-white carpet and then sucking it up with their mouths. Nope, never saw that coming.

As far as I'm concerned, life is just an exercise in constantly readjusting your expectations because nothing – no really, nothing—seems to turn out the way you dreamed it all up in your mind. The good news is this: All that disappointment isn't nearly as disappointing as you thought it was going to be. Who knew you could laugh yourself silly and burst with pride at the same time when you sit on the couch and listen to your 7-year-old son teach a Family Home Evening lesson on repentance?

"When you do something wrong, Heavenly Father wants you to repent. It makes him really happy if you repent. But it's really, really hard to repent. I mean, it's so, so hard. You have to have a whole lot of courage to repent because it's so hard. (Sees me giggling.) No, really. Repenting is really, really, really hard."

He's got a point, you know. It's not easy to admit that you're wrong about something. It's even harder to admit when you've been wrong about pretty much everything. I know because my entire motherhood journey has been rife with repentance.

I used to think that mothers should be patient and kind all the time. I also thought that people choose to be moms because they love all that kid-related stuff like play dates at the park and making your own baby food and baking cookies for the PTA. Now that I'm all grown up, I realize that really only about 1.7% of the population is actually well-equipped to be a good mother. The rest of us just kind of muddle through it somehow, despite the obvious deficiencies in our résumés.

Anyway, my life turned out different than I thought. Despite the fact that my dating life was many years of frustration dabbled with moments of humiliation, unrequited admiration, and my own episodes of Mormon-girl soap opera, I eventually found love. It actually found me because, if you reference my journals at the time, you'll know I had already surrendered myself to the solitary life I had pictured in my youth. So, yes, I fell in love. And one of the most remarkable things about falling in love is the discovery of a completely different kind of future than you'd pictured for yourself. The right person can make you see yourself doing things you never dreamed were possible. Sometimes, like in the case of having children, you never even dreamed they were desirable. But Cupid works his magic, and just like Dr. Seuss's Grinch, your heart grows two sizes.

Making the decision to start your family is no small matter. It's possible to know that something is the right thing to do and still be scared out of your mind. I never had cold feet about marrying my husband, but I fearfully tiptoed on the threshold of motherhood for years. I had faith in God and I knew He loved and honored children and families, but I didn't have faith in myself. I still stupidly thought I had to be "qualified" to be a mother. One day I realized what was probably already obvious to all the people who knew me or who had taken the leap themselves: You'll never be ready. I stopped fighting it and we moved forward.

Now I have three children who are really quite beautiful when they are sleeping. If my teenaged self had had any idea how much I would love these loud, dirty, and hyperactive little monsters, she would have started that spiral notebook and let herself dream. These children have torn me down with sleepless nights and singing in annoying voices in the car and spilled canisters of brown sugar and the artful placement of unknown substances in my carpets and on my walls. The miracle, though, is that by tearing me down, they've somehow managed to rebuild me into something I never knew I could be.

I am a mother.

I try to be patient and kind, and I probably have about a 50% success rate. I'm not fond of play dates because they unfortunately involve other people's children. I never once made my own baby food unless you count smashing up whatever was on my plate at the Cheesecake Factory (which, by the way, resulted in my plate being picked up by toddler hands and thrown into a pile of shattered pieces on the restaurant floor, followed by my son puking all over the table. True story.). I don't think I've ever baked anything for the PTA, but I was the secretary on the PTA board for one year, and managed to make a "funny" comment once that made another lady so mad she got up and left the meeting. Anyway, I've somehow managed to shatter most of the stereotypes I had about motherhood. I do it my own way, and it only works for one simple reason:

God helps me.

He lets me try again and again to get it right when I get it wrong. When I have a day full of frustration and yes, sometimes despair, He blesses me with a moment of joy or a glimpse of clarity and I know I am doing what He made me for. Even when I lose my temper because I find all the clean clothes I just folded "put away" in the dirty laundry hamper, or when I get food off the pantry shelf to make dinner and find the hidden wrappers of forbidden treats, or when I spend 45 minutes trying to convince my daughter that "my shoes feel funny" is not a sufficient reason to stay home from preschool, there is still a reassurance that it all counts. It counts for their good. It counts for my character. It matters to God. And sometimes, if I listen carefully, He reminds me.

One night my daughter woke me up to tell me she had peed in her bed. Her sheets were wet, her clothes were wet, and she was cold. I helped her change out of her clothes, washed her body with a warm washcloth, stripped the sheets, started the laundry, and tucked her into a new bed. She asked me to wrap her in the blankets "like a burrito," and I did. I kissed her on the head, she snuggled down into the mattress, smiled, and said "good night." As I walked out of the room, I turned off all the lights, and in the dark journey back to my bed, I was given some thoughts. (Because sometimes thoughts are given, not just thought.) I reflected on recent news stories of children who are abused or neglected. I thought of people in the world who would have yelled at or beaten their daughter for wetting her bed. I imagined how someone who was caught up in the after-effects of drug or alcohol use might have ignored her and left her to fend for herself or spend the night in cold, urine-soaked sheets and clothing. And in the middle of all those heavy thoughts, I felt a keen sense that my Heavenly Father was happy with how I just treated His little child. I knew He noticed it, loved it, honored it. It felt like I did exactly what the Savior would have done if he were here. I knew that my role as a mother, a woman, and a nurturer was important. But even more than important: It felt divine – God-ordained and God-beloved – even in all the apparent simplicity of the moment.

My whole life has become a collection of these simple moments, the kind of moments that my young self could never appreciate. In fact, lots of people who consider themselves adults and educated and capable don't appreciate it either. But like many truths, the truth about the divine role of women is often buried in the details of daily living and goes mostly unnoticed by the world at large.

I used to dream really big. My notebooks were more about traveling the globe and getting degrees and teaching and making a difference. And you know what? I think I have done all of those things, but not one of them matters to me as much as the dream I never dared to dream. God and my little family have turned me into a better 'me' than the 'me' I had imagined. And when all is said and done, if I found out that I wasn't allowed to keep most of the things that are important to me, my husband and children are the things I would hold on to the tightest. The things I never knew I wanted are my greatest treasure.

Hopefully my bridesmaids' dresses would be among the first things to go because, frankly, I really should have put more thought into those.

One Thing I Do Well

Becca Wilhite

It fills every room and rolls out the front door like a noxious cloud. Heavy, dark, ugly and ever-present. How is it possible that nobody else sees it? It must be my fault. If I'd taught them right, they'd see it.

It obscures the windows that haven't been washed in too many weeks. It wraps around that girl's head, the one who hasn't brushed her hair since last semester.

It drips from the kitchen table along with the sticky remnants of someone's sugar-cereal breakfast. It soaks into the towels wadded and rotting on the bathroom floor.

It's guilt, and I am really good at it.

Where does it come from? I'll tell you where it comes from. Everywhere. From the fact that I made them apple pie and called it breakfast. From my justification that "servings" of vegetables can be counted to include chocolate – because it comes out of a bean – frozen white corn, and cookies. (Vegetable oil. It says so right on the package.)

It comes from matted leaves I couldn't be bothered to rake out of flowerbeds that grow thicker grass than the lawn. From the Mount Everest of laundry, under which is the ladybug costume that somebody needs for the school program in seventeen minutes. From the dust so thick it may have actually changed the color of the carpet around the edges. It grows in the "garden" where no vegetable, not even a zucchini, will.

It comes when I realize that my kids don't know anything they need to know in order to survive Life Without Me. Including, but not limited to, how to eat, how to cook, how to clean up a bathroom floor, how to put gas in a car, how to balance a bank account, how to get out of bed in the morning, and how to complete an assignment without me pounding on the table, calling out how many minutes are left before Total Maternal Meltdown.

It comes from too many snarky comments and not enough Positive Feedback. It comes from the constant eye-roll—mine, not theirs. It comes from the frustration and the exhaustion and the grouchiness that I never quite keep hidden.

It comes because we don't have a pet. Because I won't even consider buying a pet. Not only that, I don't want the Change of Heart that would be required to ever, ever desire a pet. Because, no.

It comes when I drive past the school parking lot and see that my kid's bike is the only one, fuzzed in frost, parked in the bike rack, when every other kid got driven in a warm car. It comes when I realize that I haven't seen a single page of homework in at least six weeks. And that I can't even remember what the letters PTA stand for.

It comes when I open the fridge door to make myself some lunch and stare at all manner of colorful produce, turn up my nose, and open a bag of tortilla chips. It comes when I eat the entire contents of that bag and then chase it down with a milkshake (for protein and calcium, you know).

It comes when I sit down with a piano practicer and tell them all the things they're doing wrong. It comes double when I don't sit down with the practicer at all.

It comes from the distinction—the huge, gaping hole—between what I know I should do and what I actually manage. Between the ideal and the real. Between the hope, the desire, the wish . . . and the everyday.

It magnifies, too. It grows when the boy's hair is long and shaggy and still cute enough to be almost stylish, but hey, just too long. It grows when I buy white bread, even though there's enough wheat in the basement to bake wholesome bread for dozens of families for the foreseeable future. It grows when my fifth grader is clearly the only one who prepared her American History Wax Museum character all by herself.

It intensifies, concentrates and hovers over me on Sunday. Every Sunday. Church has its own little fog machine of guilt that sits on my shoulders when I walk into the building. It circles around my head as I let my teenagers play word-search games and draw pictures of the neighbors instead of listening to the messages. And don't even get me started on their shoes. How, how could I not have checked their feet before I let them out of the house? It presses against my ears and squeezes my brain when I glide through my church assignment instead of spending hours on my knees and on my feet preparing something phenomenal. It whispers in my ear to look at that family, the one with perfectly happy children who look actually glad to be here. To look at that one, the family with the really clean clothes that all match. To look at that one, the family whose kids are so still they might be asleep sitting up.

Worse, it whispers to look at that one, the family covered in dog hair and breakfast, and sigh, "at least that's not us." Then it multiplies exponentially, that blasted guilt, because, hello? Remember charity? Remember goodwill? Remember Kindness Begins with Me?

I'm a guilt vacuum. I can suck it up like nobody's business. But lest you fear that I'm holding it all inside, I should probably tell you that I'm equally awesome at giving it back.

Without a word, I can eke an apology from a child for any of the following: spilling something, eating too much of something, not eating enough of something, not finishing a project, forgetting to clean up after attempting to finish a project, dirty rooms, messy bathrooms, shoes on the floor, an A-minus, or missing dinner.

With only a sigh, I can spread the fog of guilt into closet corners where unused craft projects curdle. I can blow it under beds where crumbs of unknown origin molder and grow legs.

Some child development experts may tell you that babies learn to mimic smiles as their first social expressions. Not my babies. Deep sighs and eye-rolls. And how do you think I feel about that?

Give you one guess.

Emotional Wounds, Lacerations, and Internal Bleeding

Annette Lyon

G oing into parenthood, I had grand plans to be the perfect
mother. By the time my children entered school, they'd always clean up after themselves. They'd know right from wrong—
and act accordingly. They would be contributing members of
society. And of course, along the way, I'd never do anything they'd
look back on with hurt.

A perfectly good plan, in a perfect world.

A perfectly ridiculous plan in the real one.

I've learned that I can't be the perfect mother. But it wasn't
that long ago when every news report or article touting another
study about babies and children made me fret over what I'd done wrong.

It didn't matter whether it was a new food danger, a product
recall, a recently discovered household hazard, or a warning from
behavioral development experts. It didn't matter, because I'd fed
my children that exact poisonous juice in cancer-causing sippy cups

while they fried their young brains on a Disney video and then fell asleep in the range of the television's electromagnetic radiation.

Bad, bad, mommy.

I celebrated each time I managed to keep a child alive through the maze of choking hazard warnings—when they were "3+" and therefore out of at least those woods. Phew.

I used to think new parents should be given a pamphlet with basic information about this sort of thing, but because so much changes, and because no child is the same, a simple card reading, "Hey, good luck," might be just as helpful.

Even if someone managed to write a useful baby owner's manual, most parents wouldn't believe the ultimate truth anyway: no matter how hard you try to be perfect, you'll still injure each child. Multiple times. And they'll bear the scars forever.

I know I would have scoffed at the suggestion.

One thing I could have used was someone letting me in on the secret that no two children can be raised with the same method. That when you figure out how to solve a big behavioral problem with your first child don't move forward with a smug sense of, "Well, I'll totally avoid that pitfall next time."

Oh, you'll certainly avoid the same problem. But it turns out, the second child will be nothing like your first. You'll mess up just as badly as you did the last time around the track, because instead of white, horizontal hurdles, these ones will be polka-dotted cylinders.

So you'll adapt. You'll read more research and pray and study and watch your children. Your intentions will be good. Remember that when things fall apart.

Your children won't remember how you stayed up all night

when they literally turned green with a raging virus. Or all the times you cleaned up bodily fluids from every orifice—or vomited pink antibiotic liquid. Or how you stayed up until two in the morning to help with a crucial science fair project. Or practically earned his Eagle award for him. Or how you slaved over Halloween costumes to make them just perfect—which the child wore exactly once before deciding it wasn't quite what she wanted after all.

No, you'll have a child like my daughter, who instead remembers that when she was in kindergarten, I forgot to send her to school wearing green on St. Patrick's Day. How she was pinched by the entire class all day long. Naturally, their memories are infallible. The pinching wasn't just one annoying boy during a ten-minute storytelling time.

The pinching was the entire class, all day.

No wonder she came home in tears.

A few years after I'd sent this child to the wolves on St. Patrick's Day, the holiday rolled around again. Grandma Lyon sent little bracelets with green charms for the girls to wear. That morning over breakfast, I helped my daughter put on her bracelet.

As I tied it on, she piped up with, "Hey, Mom, remember the time you didn't have me wear green, and how I came home crying because I was pinched all day by my whole class, all day? Man, that was awful."

My attempt at a smile probably made me look constipated. Yes, dear. I totally remember. But I'd hoped you'd forgotten. She's now in junior high and still talks about that nightmarish day.

I think back on all the other things she doesn't remember. Like the months I walked the floor with her as a colicky baby. My only comfort was the half gallon of ice cream in the fridge. She's never wondered why we had a grocery budget to cover Rocky Road or where my addiction came from.

The worst way I scarred that pinched child was, in hindsight, somewhat preventable. But if you'd asked me in the moment who was the likely child to harbor wounds about that day, I would have picked the wrong one.

One Saturday, I was up most of the night with a heinous migraine. Sunday morning, I woke up after getting precious little sleep. I felt off-center and weak, but I had a Relief Society presidency meeting to get to. I got out of bed and got dressed in a skirt and blouse then headed to the kitchen, wondering whether eating breakfast would calm my roiling stomach or make things worse.

Seconds later, I had my answer: I rushed to the sink so I wouldn't spew stomach acid onto the kitchen floor. As I leaned over the sink, staring at the backsplash, dizziness washed over me, overwhelming the nausea.

I'm going to pass out.

The thought was clear, so even with the nausea, I figured I'd better lie down. I walked a few steps toward the great room. The couch was on the other side of the kitchen table, maybe fifteen feet away. That's all I remember, because somewhere between letting go of the sink and taking a few steps, I blacked out. I landed face first right on the seam where the kitchen tile meets the great-room carpet.

My next memory is lifting my head and seeing a puddle of red, then hearing my son say, "Mom? Mom, are you okay?"

Great.

Surely this was the child who would one day lie on a couch, recounting to a therapist how, at the tender age of twelve, he'd watched his mother die. Talk about emotional internal bleeding.

As any responsible mother lying in her own blood would do, I cheerfully assured him I was fine, then asked, "Hey, would you go get Dad?"

The girls—his younger sisters—were all still asleep, and I didn't want to wake them up only to panic them with, "By the way, I'm going to the emergency room. Ignore the blood." Besides, I figured we'd be home before they woke up anyway.

With a baseball-sized wad of red-stained toilet paper pressed against my nose, I made sure our son had our cell phone numbers. I told him not to worry about getting everyone ready for church until he heard from us.

My husband helped me into the minivan, and once I buckled my seatbelt, I lay my head back, still holding the tissues to my nose, and hoped I wouldn't pass out again—or throw up—on the way to the ER. The world swam around my head, and I could hardly see straight. But I comforted myself with the thought that at least I'd done my motherly duty by making sure my son was all right, and that my daughters would sleep through the mini crisis without unnecessary worry. Even in the fog that was my brain, I felt a bit of satisfaction for handling the situation so well.

I should have known better.

When we arrived at the hospital, they did an EKG to check for any heart problems. They x-rayed my nose to confirm that yes, it was broken in several locations, and they confirmed that my fainting was simply a result of the migraine from the night before.

The doctor said not to be alarmed if I ended up with raccoon eyes from bruising.

At one point, my husband looked at the clock in the ER and realized that we wouldn't be making it to church at all—but he was supposed to speak in sacrament meeting. He called a member of the bishopric and gave what was probably one of the best excuses for getting out of a talk: "I'm at the hospital with my wife; she broke her nose . . ."

After we got home, I rested for the remainder of the day—when I wasn't throwing up blood. My only real concern was a vain one: how bad would my eyes look? While lying in bed, I decided that hey, I could use details from the experience in a novel sometime. I knew firsthand what it's like to break your nose. (I totally used it, too; nothing is ever lost on a writer.)

Everything turned out just fine. Even my son—once he realized Mom wasn't seriously hurt—spent much of the day hanging out with his buddy Nintendo DS.

Unbeknownst to me, however, my third child—the one scarred from St. Patrick's Day—was falling apart. When I emerged from our bedroom, she pointed to her brother. "He was the only one home when I woke up. And he didn't tell me anything, just that you and Dad were at the hospital and you were hurt. I thought you were dying!"

Crud. It's one thing to forget a green t-shirt so boys won't pinch your child. It's quite another to waltz off to the hospital without realizing she may think her mother is dead.

I held her in my lap and tried to comfort her, guilt washing over me—of course, because I'm a mom. "I'm okay. I promise," I said. "Dad and I should have woken you guys up to tell you what was happening."

Except that we'd both been rushed and single-minded, and such a thing wasn't even on our radar. The perfect storm for unforgettable childhood trauma.

As I convalesced, my daughter glued paper together and drew a picture on the top and wrote a note on the bottom. The picture was of the two of us. The bottom half, in her shaky, uneven writing, read,

"Hope you fell better."

Fell, I thought. Cute. So I laughed—albeit silently. No way would I knowingly pierce her heart again.

That day was years and years ago, but I still have that note hanging on the wall beside my bedroom door. Seeing her misspelling brings a smile to my face. As I watch my daughter growing into a capable, strong, self-confident young woman, the picture is a bit of comfort that, childhood trauma notwithstanding, I haven't entirely botched this mothering thing.

When I'm presented with a parenting decision, I can think about her note and try to fall better. Not fail. No, instead I can find a delicate way of handling the situation—one better than collapsing in a pool of my own ineptitude. I thought I was doing okay on this mothering gig, having inflicted no major emotional or psychological lacerations of late. Then I told my daughter the reason I'd kept that picture hanging by the door all these years—that it was largely because of the pun with her misspelling.

She tilted her head in curiosity then ran off to read the note, now curling at the edges with age. A minute later, she returned, eyes hooded. In a total martyr tone she said, "You kept it because it's funny? And all this time I thought you saved it because it meant something to you."

Anyone have the name of a good counselor?

Why Our Family Home Evening Made Satan Happy

Stephanie Sorensen

O ne night last year, we had the worst Family Home Evening ever. Dead prophets probably rolled over in their graves. Family Home Evening is supposed to be a time where your family participates in wholesome recreation and studies some gospel principles together.

Well, we had a little bit of a sass problem that particular day, and at one point Clark even took a swing at me. This was, of course, completely unacceptable. Matt got home from work and I was exhausted. He was exhausted. We both lay down on our bed bemoaning our exhausted states. Matt suggested we have a "lying down" Family Home Evening. I knew right from the start it wasn't going to go well, but I was too lazy to get up and do anything different. (Feel free to file this in your "How to be pathetic" folder.) So we called all the kids into our room, basically to gather around our corpses and be instructed. They made paper-bag puppets of themselves and then Matt said we were going to talk about respect and responsibility. After several mind-numbing attempts to get them to define those terms, we tried to think of examples of respect from the scriptures. Clark volunteered that when Nehor killed Gideon, that wasn't very respectful. Right. This led to a long list of people beating, killing, and basically destroying one another, and pointing out as a tangent that "that wasn't respectful." I lay there (yes, lay there) rolling my eyes.

Then Matt directed a puppet show that basically re-enacted the way Clark had treated me earlier when I told him he couldn't have a play date with his friend. Unfortunately, the children thought that the representation of their previous poor behavior was hilarious. They couldn't wait until it was their turn to be the puppet and yell at and hit their mother. So our Family Home Evening turned into an unfettered, all-out paper-bag puppet brawl of people screaming at and beating on each other until the puppets lay in tattered shreds on the ground. Matt wearily tried to make a summary statement about how it's important to be respectful, and then we released our feral children to go play something else. We stood in the kitchen a few minutes later and looked at each other with dumbfounded disbelief. "That was such a bad Family Home Evening," Matt said. We tried to laugh, but we were too tired.

Elder David A. Bednar once taught: "Each family prayer, each episode of family scripture study, and each Family Home Evening is a brushstroke on the canvas of our souls. No one event may appear to be very impressive or memorable. But just as the yellow and gold and brown strokes of paint complement each other and produce an impressive masterpiece, so our consistency in doing seemingly small things can lead to significant spiritual results.

'Wherefore, be not weary in well-doing, for ye are laying the foundation of a great work. And out of small things proceedeth that which is great'1. Consistency is a key principle as we lay the foundation of a great work in our individual lives and as we become more diligent and concerned in our own homes."2

So maybe our Family Home Evening didn't really make Satan happy, because, hey, at least we tried. But it might still be the Family Home Evening that goes down in history for getting a good chuckle from both heaven and hell.

Maybe that's a masterpiece after all.

1.Doctrine and Covenants 64:33

2.Bednar, David A. "More Diligent and Concerned at Home," Ensign. November 2009.

Joshua Was a Chicken, Too

Michelle Budge

It takes courage to be single. If something needs to be done, I do it. If money needs to be made, I make it. If the car breaks down, I fix it. If I buy something at IKEA, I load it in the car and I build it. It's all up to me.

My roommate is also single, but she's not a chicken like me. She's a cop who beats up bad-guys and shoots guns. She's strong and capable. She was also out of town recently when a huge storm of hurricane-force winds blew through my area. I was in the house alone blabbing on the phone to a friend when the lights and the phone went dead. Even my mobile phone refused to work, except for a few frantic texts to my brothers. My police-officer brother Nick responded that the power company's website showed a map of power outages all over the metropolitan area. That was the last I heard from him, even though I kept hitting 'resend.'

I worried that if Nick knew the location of the power-outage, the bad-guys did too, and I hated that I was alone. There were neighbors on my street who had blazing lights and TVs only five minutes ago. But they had disappeared into the blackness. I couldn't help but notice the strobe light of the moon through the gyrating pine trees on the hill just above our house. The huge branches cracked as they were whipped by the wind. You know the Whomping Willow in Harry Potter? Right outside my door. There I was with no power, no communication and no confidence.

Thankfully that same brother had, months before, given me a 72-hour kit including a forehead-numbing headlamp, extra batteries, some gloves and Nick's favorite MREs.

Apart from strapping on the headlamp and lacing up my running shoes, I knew I was powerless to do anything. However, I did have the best communication plan that tithing and a generous fast-offering can buy. I knelt next to the backpack and poured out my soul. In a very direct and sweet heart-to-heart with my Father, I told him that I figured I'd just stay in the house, but would He please give me fair warning if a) a bad-guy showed up or b) a tree was falling my way. Then I tried to sleep, relying on the hope of 'fair warning.'

It was amazing. I should have flipped out. I could see the craziness outside. Big flashes of white light illuminated the sky as transformers blew across the city. Horrid cracking and crashing made me flinch as all hell blew loose outside. I focused on the calm feeling from the Spirit and lay down on my bed. I went to bed with my shoes on, and slept for a good four hours until a police car crept up our street shining the spotlight up in the trees, maybe looking for downed power lines. I nearly ran out there yelling "I'm alive! Help me!" But I felt that calm feeling and kept relying on 'fair warning.'

When it was light enough to see in the morning, I jumped out of bed and raced outside. (Convenient when you sleep in your clothes and shoes). I walked all around our yard and street surveying the damage. It wasn't nearly as bad as I'd imagined. Amazingly the big pine trees and their giant branches were still intact-- although twelve inches of small branches, leaves and pine needles carpeted the ground.

I decided to skip the MRE breakfast, and drove to work so I could charge all my electronics and get some email access. When I drove out of my little street over the piles of pine-cones, I burst into tears as I saw the devastation. Gigantic trees blocked nearly every street in the city. Over 1,000 trees were wiped out. 500,000 houses had lost power, and many did not get it back for a week. I didn't realize how blessed I'd been until I saw how bad everything else was. I saw how much I was protected from bad-guys and falling trees, and how I was blessed with immense courage.

Other times I am not so brave. There's this timeline issue that makes me a real chicken. The Timeline says that LDS young women may start wearing makeup at 12, go to dances at 14, date at 16, go to college at 18, and marry before graduation – for sure before slogging through Physical Science. Buy a house and have a bunch of kids. At around 45, start sending those kids out in pursuit of their own timelines. The Timeline unfairly defines me. It is not doctrine of the Church of Jesus Christ of Latter-day Saints. It's not the way to God. It's not even real. It is a misperception. However, because so many people follow The Timeline, it appears to be doctrine, the only way to be safe.

If The Timeline is normal, my timeline is abnormal. I skirted milestones along The Timeline, wishing to have dating woes at 16, and to be so busy dating in college that I failed Physical Science. I wished and prayed to get married and have a bunch of kids before I was 40. Instead, my timeline was all jumbled. I finished college, then worked, then went to more college. Then worked some more. I am still working. And I'm still not married. Though I am pretty blessed and downright happy, the fear and dismay of being abnormal according to The Timeline often stops me from moving forward. It makes me fear living in certain areas where I may be the only old, weird single sister. It makes me hesitate to buy a house because The Timeline says you do that after you're married. It makes me lie about my over-forty age to lessen the shocked response, "and still not married?!"

It takes courage to be single. But, it takes more courage to trust in the Lord and to follow His will. It takes courage to really let Him run the show. I am used to running my own show. And the Lord's timeline doesn't look that great from here. Because it requires faith to travel on this odd and unexpected path, I search the scriptures for similar people who struggle. A favorite character is Joshua —and not because he was so handsome in The Ten Commandments. I like Joshua because he was one big chicken. He got comfy letting Moses handle all the stress. But after Moses died, he found himself with a new calling. This was game time: Cross a big river with a zillion people, and all their animals and stuff—and then take over a country. These responsibilities would require their own, separate miracles.

Instead of jumping right to work, he stood on the banks of

the Jordan River wringing his hands and stewing over his inad-
equacies. The Lord had to tell him three times in four verses not
to worry, that he could do this. He also blasted Joshua's negative
self-talk (and sense of alone-ness) with this scripture I read every
morning: "Be strong and of a good courage, be not afraid neither
be thou dismayed: for the Lord thy God is with thee whithersoever
thou goest."

I have had awful Joshua moments; standing on the banks of
an endeavor or a trial wringing my hands in fear and dismay.

A few years ago I had the best job ever. I was a freelance
graphic designer working in a penthouse apartment next to French
doors that overlooked the treetops. I emailed my work to the office
and occasionally drove in for meetings or work sessions. I worked
for a fantastic creative director. We produced inspired, exciting design projects. Then one day my boss lost his job and everything
changed. The big boss offered me my former boss's job—with the
understanding that I commute the long distance each day to be in
the office. It was a great promotion for me, but way out of my skill-
set, with a lot of account management, business savvy, and horrid
hours. I hated it.

I feared that if I didn't take the job, I'd lose my fabulous gig.
If they hired a new creative director, he'd bring in his own free-
lancer and I'd be out. As a result of the fear and stress and work, I
got sick, got pinkeye and even got chest pains from the anxiety. I
prayed constantly throughout the days for help and somehow lasted
six months.

Finally, I couldn't handle it anymore and asked the big boss
if we could talk. Just before our meeting, I shut my office door and

knelt in front of it to pray. I pleaded with the Lord to help me say the right things so I could keep my old job, but find a new solution for the creative director position. Over the past couple of weeks I'd been formulating a plan and had reviewed it with the Lord. It all seemed good. As I prayed, I remembered the words, "all things work together for good to them that love the Lord" and I felt comfort like a blanket wrapped over my back.

I took a big breath and sported that spiritual blanket into the big boss's office and started to present my plan. I felt so confident that I didn't notice the meeting beginning to fall apart. I couldn't process the big boss getting upset and attacking my plan. I was stunned as he said that "some people just couldn't handle the corporate world." I wondered what happened to 'all things working together for good.'

Back in my office I tried to figure out how to become invisible . . . and how to find my résumé. However, two hours later, the big boss came in and apologized. He said he was taken off guard and flew off the handle. Evidently my plan had touched on key changes he planned for the department and had pre-empted his unveiling. It shocked him and he overreacted. After apologizing he blew me away with, "I'd like you to choose the new creative director."

All things did work together for my good. I am now back in my groove. The big boss and I made up and are better friends than before. And I hired a friend from school to be my new boss.

When I think about how the Lord has run to my rescue in past trials and answered past prayers, I feel foolish for being concerned about my continuing status as a single person. Like being alone in a storm, I discover how much I'm being protected only when I step outside and see the destruction everywhere around me. From surviving ninety-eight different roommates to needing an apartment and being handed a mansion, the Lord has consistently over-delivered.

It takes courage to believe that the Lord is in charge when the wind blows and trees fall, when the big boss yells, or when The Timeline seems off. But in all the best stories from the scriptures, I'm reminded I can expect a miracle. Maybe even an Old Testament-level miracle.

I remember that when the world's power went out, His power was enough to see me through.

Picking Daisy

Patrick Livingston

Miracles happen in every single adoption. Although I'm sure people who can whip up their own babies in their own bellies think that's a miracle, too, I just don't know much about it. Any adoptive parent will tell you the little things they couldn't see in the moment that turned out to be game-changers. Our adoption had a few game-changers that forever stunted my ability to question the Lord, which, up to that point, had been one of my greatest, most practiced abilities.

Our first miracle was accidentally not living in New York City. We tell people we worked in NYC and usually leave it at that, but the whole truth is that we lived in New Jersey. I know. It's like the opposite of New York City. Lindsay was getting her Ph.D. on 34th street in NYC (you know, where a different miracle happened, and the where Empire State Building is, and the Thanksgiving Day

Parade marches down), and I was working on the Upper East Side, but when you tell someone in Utah that you lived in New Jersey and worked in New York City, most people don't get it—like saying, "I work in Salt Lake, but I live in Wyoming."

Mind you, living in NYC was the plan; we never, ever thought we'd choose Hoboken, New Jersey, over Brooklyn or the Bronx, or . . . well, not the Bronx, but Queens! But five years before we adopted, five years before the miracle showed itself, we found ourselves staying (by the sheer generosity of total strangers) in a lovely one-bedroom apartment in Hoboken, New Jersey, and fell in love with this little city of brownstones on the Hudson River that looks out at the New York skyline.

The train went straight from Hoboken under the river to 34th Street in about 14 minutes, and was much closer than anything we could have found in any of the boroughs. It felt super New York-y; from my kitchen window I could see both the Statue of Liberty and the Empire State Building. It was a beautiful place to live, and we thought it was a marketing ploy when a realtor walked us down Garden Street—a quaint, quiet street lined with Sesame Street stoops, trees, parks, and people—people with strollers! (When you're looking for a safe place to live, look for people with strollers).

But it wasn't a trick: There, near 6th and Garden and kitty-corner from a little brown church, was a red-brick brownstone with a black and white awning over the front door.

We'd looked at apartments in the city, to both our deep and profound disappointment. In one-studio apartment, Lindsay told the realtor, "We have a queen-size bed," to which he responded, "Well, that's not going to fit in here!"

But this little studio was so sweet and so clearly waiting for us that we jumped at the chance and snatched it up. We considered ourselves lucky to have found an apartment. Lucky, that is, until one night, right after we moved in, when Lindsay sat bolt upright in bed and said, "Do you think I'm going to have to pay out-of-state tuition?"

I (of course) responded, "No."

After all, we lived 14 minutes away from her school. How much closer could we get? Turns out, she was right. She had a full fellowship, but it only covered in-state tuition, which meant we had to pay the difference for the next four years—a crushing blow.

Living in New York is super expensive, more than you might think: our 400-square foot studio on Garden Street (meaning no bedroom) was $1400 per month, more than my brothers' combined Utah home mortgages at the time. What's more, when any person who lived by us found out what we paid (because on the East Coast you talk freely about how much stuff costs), they told us what an amazing deal we were getting for "all that space." Our apartment even had a small porch and a yard out back, a rarity in the city.

To add the extra expense only because it didn't occur to us to find out about tuition before we signed the lease was a big blow, both financially and spiritually. I remember praying and asking why things had gone down that way; it would have been so easy just plant the thought.

Plant it, nothing! I sincerely felt we had been prevented from thinking about the tuition until the day after we moved in. My wife is a brilliant, list-keeping, file-cabinet owning woman; for her to just not think of such a simple thing as "live in the state in which you go to school" was strange, and I didn't like the interference – or lack of it – from above. But, in my regular routine of questioning the Lord, I was given a quiet little witness that it was because of our baby.

That was almost six years before we adopted. At the time, I believed it meant we'd find our baby in New Jersey. This was not to be, but we did find our ward (the greatest one ever assembled). We found friends we would have for the rest of our lives. The remainder of our first miracle would come later.

Our second miracle was Kim, the 22-year-old white girl from Sandy, Utah. Long before Lindsay and I met, I worked in a law office with a woman who had adopted an African-American baby boy. She told me the statistics for black children being adopted, and they broke my heart. An African-American boy over the age of three has the least chance of any child of being adopted into a home, which means that, instead of being raised by a loving family, he'll likely be passed around foster care for 15 years until he's legally old enough to be on his own. By age three, his life was pretty much decided for him. I don't even remember being three, let alone it having determined the rest of my childhood and beyond. I knew then that I'd adopt and that my kids would have dark skin.

Then I met Lindsay, who had known since she was 13 that her body couldn't whip up babies, and I remembered the witness I'd had in the law office. I knew we'd have a little multicolored family.

So, when birthmother Kim showed up, she was . . . well, white. In our minds, our babies had always been black. But we'd been waiting to be parents for years, and hers was the only baby coming our way. As adoptive parents, you really do believe that you don't have the right to turn down any baby. We were also working with LDS Social Services, so we had faith that God would send us a baby on His timeline. This was a baby, so it must have been the one, even if it didn't fit the witness we had had before.

Kim had found herself pregnant and not in love with the baby's father. She found us on the Church's adoption website. She was very direct with us, and that made her sort of funny. Lindsay and Kim started communicating quickly, and Kim hatched a plan to come out to meet us in New York. Both her caseworker and ours strongly discouraged what could be a highly emotional—and potentially awkward—situation. Usually when—if—birthmothers meet adoptive couples, it's done at a lunch, with both caseworkers at the table holding 3x5 cards with interesting, inoffensive topics that can be discussed.

But we invited Kim to fly to New York and stay at our house. How bad could it be? She was a pregnant 22-year-old; if it came to a fight, Lindsay could probably take her. Actually, the visit went just fine, although thinking back on it, we took quite a risk. Adoption is full of horror stories of people scamming other people, sometimes not even for money, but just for the fun of it. For that matter, we could have been crazy people who'd toss her in a closet and wait for the baby to come.

Our caseworkers told us that if we were going to go through with this visit, we could not give her one cent. We weren't allowed to pay for her meals or buy her souvenirs; even giving her a place to stay was questionable. If a judge thought for one moment that we "bought" a baby from this girl, we would lose the baby—and go to jail. So Kim would have to buy her own Empire State Building snow globe. She was sweet and funny and asked us questions about our TV watching habits, music and food tastes. She was nervous and compensated by being thorough in her questioning, as she should have been.

She was only five weeks along, meaning that we'd all be in this pregnancy together for the long haul. She told us upfront that she was choosing between us and another couple who already had children. I wasn't worried; we were the ultra-cool, New York City couple with the cutest apartment in the cutest building. We didn't have any kids, and those other people already had some. What did they need more for? And we were the cutest, funniest, most accomplished, talented couple on the whole Church adoption website—at least, so said my mother, and she should know; she looked at the site three times a day for a year and a half.

We had a great time in the city with Kim. We went to the Met and Central Park. We spent lots of time talking and laughing and walking and thinking. After two days, we drove her back to the airport, but I wouldn't put her on the plane without getting some sort of hint as to her intentions.

"So . . . how are you doing?" I asked.

"Fine," she said. "Tired."

"Yeah, sure, of course. . . . And, um . . . what are you thinking? About . . . you know, the baby?" Lindsay gave me a look that I ignored.

"I don't know," Kim replied. "I've still got to think about things, I'm just so tired right now."

Granted, she was seven weeks pregnant, and we'd dragged her all over New York City. She'd slept in a strange house on a strange couch, and she definitely had a lot to think about.

But that was it, right there. I remember it so clearly: I looked at Lindsay. And she knew, and I knew, and we both knew that we knew: it wasn't gonna happen. We were never going to be better, or funnier, or cooler than we were while she was right here, and if she didn't know that we were the right family for her baby right now, she never would.

Driving home from the airport, after dropping off the only person in nearly two years who'd even considered our parenting skills, we felt this huge weight of "square one" settle on our chests. It was too much for Lindsay, and even though she could feel that Kim's baby was not ours, the whole idea of going back to the waiting, and not hearing, and never knowing, was just too much. This, at least, had been something. It had started as an email from the agency, then an email from a birthmother, then a phone call, then travel plans, and then a face-to-face, three-day weekend, then a car ride home. And in that car ride, we knew we were back to nothing.

Except, that wasn't really true, because there was Daisy.

When we drove Kim to the airport, Daisy was seven months baked in someone else's belly, waiting for us to get our act together and find her.

We got home from the airport and called an old friend— rather, a girl I'd dated a few times eight years ago. We'd parted on reasonably good terms, and she'd since adopted three African-American children. This type of connection becomes your finding pool; anyone you ever knew, or sort of knew, or are kind of related to, suddenly becomes a person you can call out of the blue and say, "Hey, tell us about your precious little family and how we can get one . . . not yours, but our own."

Luckily, the other side of the coin is that people who have adopted are usually more than willing to talk about it. Using strangers' helping hands is a hard thing and we've all been there. So I Facebooked my friend, and she was a well, a deep well with sayings we'd later vinyl on the walls of our house. She advised us on the pros and cons of working with LDS Social Services. She helped us understand the financial help available to adoptive families. And she assured us that it was all right to have some idea of what we hoped our baby would be. We will always be grateful for her insights and direction.

At first I felt that I'd been lazy or distracted to have taken so long to find our baby. But then I had this overwhelming feeling that our baby wasn't on the earth yet, and that babies don't come and sit on the shelf until you're ready. They come when you are ready.

And—suddenly and finally—we were.

About six weeks after we took Kim to the airport, we were in a hospital in Payson, Utah, giving our daughter Daisy her first bath. She was exactly who we had always pictured when we thought about our family.

I want to say that I knew she was ours right from the start, but when you adopt, there's this room in your heart, way toward the back, where you have to put the one doubt—that single doubt that this whole thing might fall apart and you'll be left with a loss. You put that thought deep in a room and lock it away, and then you go on acting like the room doesn't exist, because you don't want to miss out on the fun part of buying her clothes and selecting a bed skirt or choosing her name.

But when I saw Daisy, I wanted our child to be her. Every

part of me ached for this to be the real thing. She was perfect and soft and pink (yes, pink) and she was sleeping and smiling. A line was crossed, and the locked-up room in my heart was abandoned. From then on, even if things had fallen apart, she still would have been ours, if only for that time.

She still would have been ours.

But things didn't fall apart, and they never will. The government says she's ours, and Heavenly Father sealed her to us forever. Sitting in the hospital, waiting for Daisy to arrive, we talked to our caseworker about how funny it was that she would be born in Utah, and all the ups and downs of our little adoption.

She said, "I know. When I saw that you worked in New York City, I pulled this birthmother from your list, because New York State doesn't allow out-of-state adoptions. But then I saw that your home address was in New Jersey, which is open to any adoption. So it was no big deal."

We found our baby, who could never have been ours if we had lived 14 minutes to the left, across the river, in New York City.

No big deal? Maybe.

A miracle? Definitely.

Deaf Branch

Melanie Jacobson

Once, I almost had a transcendent experience. The heavens-parting kind.

I was seventeen, and for about ninety seconds, it was mind-blowing. I was sitting in the chapel, zoning out on the speaker at the pulpit, when I heard this: "Ahhhh, ahhhh, ahhhhhhhh..." A string of notes, quiet, but a stark contrast to the usual chapel sounds. I looked around, but everyone else had their eyes on the speaker, pretending to listen to him. It came again, a rising scale of beautiful notes in a sweet soprano. "Ahhhh, ahhhh, ahhhhhhhh..."

I sat up straighter, craning to locate the source. Nothing seemed out of place. No one else seemed to notice. My mom shot me a funny look, but it didn't stop me from twisting and turning on the pew to locate the angelic singing. There, again! "Ahhhh, ah-hhh, ahhhhhhhh..."

Could this be the ministering angels spoken of in scripture? Is that why only I heard them? Granted, half the adults in the chapel were deaf, but even the hearing ones didn't seem to notice. It was freaky. Why could only I hear it? And if it was an angel, um...what did that mean? I'm sure as a Primary kid I must have thought seeing an angel would be cool, like maybe it would come visit me and pet me like a puppy and let me fly around with it. But as a teenager, any angels coming to visit were probably the variety who dropped in on Laman and Lemuel and Alma the Younger and Saul of Tarsus. I definitely did not want any of those angels coming to see me, but there it was again: "Ahhhh, ahhhh, ahhhhhh..."

It came from the middle pew on the far side of the chapel, an awfully specific origin point for a heavenly host. I stared harder and tuned the speaker out as I waited for it again. And when at last it came, there was good news and bad news, and it was the same news for both: it wasn't an angel.

It was a little girl with a talking Ariel doll from The Little Mermaid. It sang each time she pressed a button in the doll's back.

On the one hand, relief washed over me. No angel would be dropping any hard assignments in my lap that day. ("Go forth and bear a half-human, half-God in the stable of an inn.") I also wasn't about to be called to repentance. ("Seriously, the Father says stop beating on your brother and sister. Listen, because His punishments are way worse than your dad's.") On the other hand, I wasn't going to be flying around the skies or getting an angel hug, which is a thing I invented in my head as a kid but which sounded like the best hug ever. And since I didn't really let my parents hug me anymore, an angel hug would have been nice.

No, I was having the same experience as half the congregation of listening to plastic Ariel, only they ignored it. I couldn't ignore it any more than I could ignore the dozen other bright shiny things that distracted me on a daily basis.

Bummer.

Of course, if it had been a normal congregation, the toy would never have made it through the oak double doors. But like I said, half of the people in the chapel were deaf. The parents sitting on the row with the Ariel-toting little girl had their eyes fixed on the sign language interpreter standing next to the speaker, soaking up some religion through her signs. They had no idea that the little mermaid could sing. I mean, it's a mermaid. I'm sure they figured on their child brushing the doll's lush nylon locks, not using it to almost visit a life-changing experience on an inattentive teenage girl during sacrament services.

Ariel stopped singing after a couple of more times. Some other adult must have explained to the parents that it was noisy. Hearing adults have to do that a lot in deaf congregations, because the noisiest place on the planet on any Sunday morning is a Mormon deaf ward or branch.

It's been years since I attended one. Ten, maybe. By the time I left for college, I was so over being in a deaf branch that I would have been happy never to set foot in another one of their sacrament meetings again. It's not easy to be part of a deaf branch. That was the hard thing to explain to my hearing friends who envied my ease with sign language or the novelty of signing all of our hymns.

It. Is. Not. Easy.

And it's not fun. CODAs, or Children of Deaf Adults, grow up interpreting for our parents in all kinds of situations. We're good at it. We know Church vocabulary especially well. And after twenty years of mixed families (hearing and deaf) coming through the branch, some of the CODAs who now had families of their own stuck their necks out for the CODAs still in the youth program.

"Don't use them as interpreters," they would admonish the branch leadership. "Let them be kids. Let them enjoy themselves. Quit making them work."

To be fair, the leadership avoided using us kids whenever they could. They'd begun to see burnout, kids who flatly refused to come back even for visits after leaving the nest, for fear of being sucked back in to interpret. As a result, they tried to use adults whenever possible.

And the thing is that sometimes kids are self-centered. I could be that way. Often. Way too often. Sometimes I'd go to youth conference and feel all inspired to help my deaf peers enjoy the experience. The idea is that serving them by interpreting and helping them to communicate should enhance my own experience, right? Sometimes, yes. But not always. That's why a lot of the youth hated doing it, pulling double duty and interpreting for the deaf youth.

I think that's what surprises people the most. It seems like if you're serving others then you should have all these blessings showering down on you, but that's not the case. It wasn't true at youth conference. It wasn't true on Sundays. Deaf members of the church felt it was their right to fully participate in meetings and lessons via interpreters, but they kind of took it for granted that we would be glad to jump in and help. And we were, mostly. But it's nice to be appreciated and often . . . we weren't.

Hence the reason the older, seasoned CODAs kept trying to run interference for us. But there were times when it would require one of us to do the job, and then we pressured each other. We got mad at each other if someone flatly refused to interpret, because it meant the burden fell to someone else. And the thing is, we were all fluent in ASL, but that doesn't make you a good interpreter right off the bat. Deaf members complained about our signing style, or other people fluent in ASL might correct our signs or dispute an interpretation. It was annoying to be criticized for doing something we didn't feel like doing anyway.

This makes the deaf people, like my parents, sound so rotten, I'm sure. They weren't, of course. This was a single aspect of the deaf branch experience. But it's one that stands out in my mind along with the memories of the loudest sacrament meetings ever. Just imagine if half of your ward never shushed their kids during the sacrament.

And yet...

I kind of miss those days. Not enough to repeat the experience, but in hindsight, I better understand the things I learned. Some are hard lessons, like just because you serve it doesn't mean that people will thank you. And service isn't always fun.

But I think back further, to before the deaf branch days, when we lived in Louisiana during my childhood and my parents were the only deaf Mormons. Sunday after Sunday, they hauled us to church to sit for three hours in meetings where they didn't know what was being said half the time. My dad spent most of those years in the bishopric, where he had to sit behind the speakers in sacrament meeting so he couldn't even lip read. But never once did my parents say, "We'll drop you off and see you when church is done because there's nothing there for us." They stuck it out for over a decade because they wanted us to have that structure and those blessings in our lives.

When we moved to California, a driving factor was the opportunity to attend the deaf branch as a family so we could all participate. My parents never complained about the quality of the interpretation. They knew what years of being without interpreters on Sundays felt like. Their biggest frustration was with deaf members who were so dependent on others for everything that they didn't take the initiative to learn and internalize the gospel for themselves.

One of my dad's greatest pet peeves was the deaf members who didn't read the Book of Mormon because they complained that it was "too hard." My dad advocated loudly—and often undiplomatically—that the needs of the deaf members be met within the stake, to make sure there was full inclusion for the deaf in everything. But he never overlooked the reality that no matter who you are or what your situation is, not everything about the gospel can be done for you.

When he became branch president, the first deaf branch president in nearly twenty years, he pushed the deaf members far harder than any hearing branch president could to take responsibility for themselves and their gospel education.

Now, as I consider the sum total of that experience, I know what I took away: not to take the gospel for granted. Not to get so bogged down in my own issues that I take the people trying to serve me for granted. Not to expect anyone to give me my testimony.

And the lessons from the things I miss now—those stick with me too. I miss interpreting talks sometimes. I hated the pressure of getting it right, but I loved the way interpreting forced me to consider the principles being taught. I had to take a word-based message and convey it as a concept, a word picture, instead. Even when I watched other interpreters and disagreed with their interpretation, it challenged me to consider the heart of the message being spoken.

I miss how beautiful a song looks when it is signed. I miss seeing my mom lead the music as if it were a dance, her hands shaping the air as gracefully as a bird lighting on a tree branch, or the wind bending grass. She could conjure an image so beautifully in the way she approached the music. A chorister in deaf branch sacrament meetings doesn't wave their hands to keep time; he or she takes on the responsibility of choosing the signs for each hymn, then the whole congregation copies the interpretation. And the choristers are almost always deaf. A hearing person stands to the side and points to the words so the chorister can keep pace with the music.

I miss the gladness on the faces of the deaf when a hearing person attempts to sign, no matter how haltingly. I miss the quick, nimble fingers of the little kids flying so confidently through the silent language. I miss being with other CODAs, who understand how growing up in deaf culture defines you as distinctly as any other culture you can name.

I miss listening to the gospel stripped down to its simplest, purest concepts to meet the comprehension levels of the deaf people who struggled with multiple learning impediments. I miss that a lot. I so often make the gospel more complicated than it needs to be, more complicated than it actually is.

Twenty years down the road, I know that I had many transcendent experiences in my deaf branch years, but they were much quieter than the ethereal Ariel song rising up from the pews that day. They were little moments of grace when I got hauled up to interpret, and by the Spirit I found a way to explain big, majestic ideas so that even the most uneducated brothers and sisters watching could understand. I found a way to explain those things so that I could understand.

Maybe that's why I still make my way to a chapel every Sunday, two decades later. Letting my hands shape ideas for those members helped me to put form to the truth, and it sticks with me. It always will.

SECTION THREE

"*If so many men, so many minds, certainly
so many hearts, so many kinds of love.*"

Leo Tolstoy

I'm His Dad

Josh Bingham

When my middle son, Noel, turned five, my wife and I decided to let him have a party with friends. It would be his first party with guests other than family members. He chose a dinosaur theme, picked out the cake, and talked about nothing else for weeks leading up to the big day.

On the day of the party, Noel seemed anxious and restless. As soon as each guest arrived, Noel wanted to open whatever present they brought. We tried explaining that we weren't opening presents until the end of the party, which brought on tears and frustration. Finally we relented; he could open the presents first, but only after everyone arrived. While the guests played games in the other room, Noel paced back and forth in front of the front window.

Finally the last guest arrived, and Noel was allowed to open his gifts. He tore through them with the enthusiasm that only a five-year old can muster. After ripping off the paper from each gift, he reluctantly said "thanks" and immediately tore into the next one. When there was nothing left to open, Noel left the party and went up to his bedroom. I was embarrassed. My son was so greedy and ungrateful; where had I gone wrong as a parent? Didn't he see how rude he was being?

We bribed and cajoled, and finally got him back downstairs. As the party progressed, Noel was miserable. He didn't like the games. He was angry when the piñata wouldn't break open on the first try. He grew bored painting rocks to look like fossils. He had some moments of elation, like when everyone sang to him and he got to blow out his candles, but for the most part, he seemed angry, unsettled and sad.

As the party finally drew to a close and we sent the other kids home, my wife and I were left frustrated and exhausted. As the last little boy walked out the door, Noel turned to us with a big grin on his face and said, "That was the best day ever!"

We were stunned. Had he been at a different party than we had? The last two hours had been torture for us. Noel had seemed to hate every minute of it.

When Noel was about two, his pediatrician suspected that he had Sensory Processing Disorder and referred us to an occupational therapist. Parts of the diagnosis seemed to fit: Since birth, Noel had trouble with loud noises and crowds. He was sensitive about what clothes he wore, insisting that some common items were too uncomfortable. Even so, we weren't convinced the diagnosis was entirely accurate, so we sort of pushed it to the back of our minds.

But about ten days after his party, Noel went in for his annual checkup. My wife discussed some of her concerns with the pediatrician, including some of the things we had observed at the party and over the last several months.

She told him how, at preschool, Noel refused to get off the bottom of the slide, then kicked the teacher when she tried to remove him. Or how once, when his classmates walked in a line holding onto a rope, Noel jerked the rope hard enough that it almost knocked a girl over. He hated taking turns, struggled with transitions and was impatient.

That day, the pediatrician told us he suspected that Noel had Asperger's Syndrome.

Asperger's Syndrome is on the autism spectrum. It's typically characterized by difficulty communicating and socializing with others. Kids with Asperger's see the world through a literal lens and have trouble understanding nuance, demonstrating flexibility, and adapting to new or unfamiliar situations. While Asperger's is more understood now than it was a generation ago, people still give you a bit of a blank stare when they hear about it. Noel is not retarded— and really, can we just do away with that word all together? And he isn't Rainman, either. He's not stupid. His intelligence is not developmentally delayed at all.

Going through the ups and downs since his diagnosis has been a tough couple of years. We have extended periods with Noel where everything is great—he's funny, loving and affectionate. He's empathetic and doesn't like to see other kids get in trouble.

But he can also be challenging. He has a terrible time grasping abstract concepts like time, so if we promise to do something "later" he demands to know exactly when "later" is and how long it'll take until that happens. And then he'll say that "later" is, in fact, forever.

Noel likes patterns and predictability, and when those patterns are interrupted, he can get incredibly upset. He's particular about what he eats and what he wears and what he likes. I can see the side-eye we get from good-natured loved ones and friends who don't believe us when we tell them Noel simply won't eat a certain food. No amount of bribing, threatening, or cajoling will work. We aren't lazy parents who give in; if he doesn't want to wear or eat or do something, you won't win the battle.

A fantastic show on NBC called Parenthood deals with a couple whose son has just been diagnosed with Asperger's. In one episode, the dad, when asked how he is doing, says "I'm angry all of the time, and then I'm mad that I feel angry."

When I heard that, it rang so true, it was scary. My patience as a father has been tested beyond what I knew it could be. I have a short-fused temper that I didn't know existed. Being the father of a child with special needs requires a lot of patience, understanding and sympathy.

And as any parent knows, at the end of a long day, the patience, understanding and sympathy tanks are often empty. But I have to constantly focus on staying positive and calm, because any negativity or anger quickly sends Noel on a downward spiral that's tough to pull him out of. We do a lot of tag team parenting.

In spite of how hard it gets, sometimes we find ourselves compelled to reassure everyone that we're doing just fine. Life isn't harder—just different! Like many parents of children with special needs, we want to look like we have it all under control. "No, everything's okay," we want to say. "We're doing great!"

And some days it's true; we are doing great. As a parent, I hope and believe that eventually the under-control days will outnumber the out-of-control days. But there are also times when you feel one step behind before you even get out of bed, and you do everything you can to hold it together. I owe a lot to my wife, who spends a lot more time on the front lines than I do. I don't know how she does it.

I realize, of course, that having a son with Asperger's is not the end of the world. A lot of parents have children who are sick or dying, and my heart aches for those moms and dads. Our situation isn't grave, but it can be tough. I know for myself that it's critical for me to live in ways that bring the Spirit into my life and into my home.

When I'm not doing what I know I should be—praying regularly, reading scriptures—my boat is more easily rocked. I wish knowing that would make it easier for me not to be too lazy or too tired to read or pray. It doesn't always. But I try to be a better person, because I know I need God on my side to make the right decisions and be the right father to Noel and my other children.

One thing I do hold onto is something powerful that my friend Rebecca told me. She has multiple special-needs kids. When we were still in the diagnosis process, I reached out to her. She told me, "A diagnosis is just a word on a piece of paper. Your son is the same person today as he was before this diagnosis. The word doesn't change that. But you and your wife were given stewardship over him by a loving Heavenly Father. You are the perfect people to help guide him though his life."

As I think back on that birthday party a year ago—and what I now understand about Asperger's—I'm amazed it didn't go worse.

Noel craves structure, routine and stability, and that birthday party had anything but. It was full of surprises, which a typical kid might love at a birthday, but which for Noel was unsettling. His sixth birthday party was much different—just family. Noel knew ahead of time what the sequence of events would be. We opened gifts at the beginning and left lots of wiggle room to adapt to his mood. And it was great. Not perfect, but better. We're still learning.

Noel is, in a word, fantastic. He's funny and smart and affectionate and my little buddy. He recently joined a t-ball team, which we would have never thought possible a year ago. He loves hitting and running—a situation where he is in control of what happens—and hates playing in the outfield—where he doesn't understand why the ball won't just come to him.

Asperger's is a piece of the pie that makes Noel who he is. And while I sometimes wish life could be "easier," I don't know that I'd want him to be different. He teaches me patience and love and understanding every day.

And, at the end of the day, I am his Dad. And I love him.

Special Occasions

Jana Winters Parkin

When I picked up our seven-year-old daughter after the first day at her new school, I was relieved to see her running up to the car bursting with wonder.

"Mommy, mommy!" She could barely contain the excitement as she announced, nearly breathless from running, "We have Special Occasions at Loma Alta!"

"Whoa! That sounds fun," I responded. "Was today a special occasion?" Jordan nodded, looking a tad confused.

"What do they do for the special occasions?" I asked, trying to understand what she was so excited about.

"Well, today the third grade Special Occasion had music," she replied.

"Oh, good! Maybe you'll get to do music too. Do they have special occasions in second grade too?" She nodded, with some hesitation. "What else do they do for the special occasions? Bring treats?"

"Yes...maybe...I guess." She paused. Then smiled. "And also I like to push them on the swings and help them tie their shoes."

Now I was the one who was looking confused.

"It's only for the kids who are Special. Some are blind, some can't hear, and some are like Jonathan." (Jonathan is our delightful friend in Pasadena who has Down Syndrome.)

"You mean the kids with special needs?"

"Yeah, that's it − Special Needs. They're the ones that go to Special Occasion."

That is the best euphemism I've ever heard for Special Education.

When I dropped her off the next morning, there was a group of kids with special needs disembarking at the bus stop.

"See, Mom? Those are the Special Occasions!"

Awesome.

Jordan likely inherited her delight over these gentle souls from her father. While I tend to be a little bit shy and more reserved, my husband Jeff is far more outgoing, and never hesitates to make a connection.

Jeff will see our friend Jonathan at church (even if a whole year's gone by) and instantly have him bursting in laughter with a mere look or gesture, reminding him of a private joke they share. I see the two of them chortling together and wonder if it's a guileless innocence they recognize in each other, or pure silliness that binds them together. Either way, what they have, what they share, is a gift.

Our daughter seems to have her own version of that same gift. Now well into her teenage years, she has retained her sense of wonder and joy over discovering someone different from her, someone who might welcome a little more nurturing and assistance.

Consider this recent conversation:

Jordan: "Mom, they put me in Special Ed Seminary!"

Me, slightly concerned: "Were you not doing okay in regular seminary?"

Jordan, not offended, even laughing a little: "They asked me to help with Special Ed seminary. We get to go to the Special Ed room, pick up the kids who want to take seminary, hold their hands and walk them up the hill to the seminary building. In the class we sing songs with them and help them participate in the lesson. Then we walk them (or push their wheelchairs) back to the Special Ed room."

Perfect.

Jordan often regales us with her Special Occasion stories at the dinner table: "They assigned me to the cutest girl, named Claire. She has Down Syndrome. Sometimes she has these stubborn and grumpy days where I'll suggest, 'Let's open your hymnbook' and she'll shake her head and mumble in a gruff little-old-man voice, 'Not today.' 'Can you fold your arms for the prayer?' 'Not today.' 'Do you need to go to the bathroom?' 'Not today.' As soon as seminary's over I say, 'Claire it's time for lunch.' Claire yells, 'Pizza!' and runs down the hill so fast I can barely catch her!"

The way our daughter describes these scenarios is every bit as joyful and celebratory as it was when she was seven.

Jordan has even recruited a few friends to join her in Special Ed Seminary because she genuinely loves it there, loves the people she serves, and wants to share the experience. To her, it's just about the best place in the world. Her friend Josh, one of Jordan's recruits, recently bore his testimony in our ward, rejoicing over the opportunity to help out in Special Ed Seminary, and declared, "Those kids have taught me, helped me and blessed me way more than I've been able to help them."

If only we could all see the differences in others the way Jordan does—as a Special Occasion, a cause for celebration—the world would be a kinder, safer, happier place.

For everybody.

There's No Price Tag on Happiness

Jana Winters Parkin

O nce, without even trying, we made a grown man cry.
During our starving-student years, while my husband, Jeff,
was studying screenwriting at USC, he decided to take a part-time
job working for a crusty old mega-millionaire who fancied himself
a filmmaker.

Curmudgeon might be too nice a word for this guy. We'll call
him Ron. He'd successfully alienated a series of ex-wives, all of his
children, and most of his employees. Now all he had was a couple of
reluctant grandkids—and Jeff—to buy the fishing poles for the next
obligatory outing.

Ron was the kind of guy who shopped at those appointment-
only boutiques in Beverly Hills, where all the staff knew him by
name. Four hundred dollars later, he'd come away with an orange
polyester turtleneck. Too much money, not enough taste. He lived in

a high-rise penthouse on Wilshire Boulevard, and had his own limos and personal driving staff. He ate nearly every meal in restaurants like Chasens and Ma Maison, and burned through money like it was trash.

Jeff came home with hilarious horror stories of Ron throwing a tantrum at work, excoriating the staff with a string of profanity, firing people on the spot, and then begging them to come back after he regained his sanity.

I frequently asked Jeff why he stayed there. Surely there was other part-time work to be found. His remarkable answer said so much about Jeff: "I kind of feel sorry for Ron." After one particularly bad Ron day, Jeff came home with the news that he'd invited Ron over for dinner.

"To our house?" The response flew out of my mouth. We lived in a one-bedroom house-above-a-garage in the heart of South-Central Los Angeles . . . in the Crenshaw District, as it was known to the locals. We affectionately referred to it as the ghetto. We had bars on all our doors and windows, recognized which ice cream truck was used for drug deals—it came around after dark playing "Strangers In the Night"—and were starting to get used to the police helicopters and drive-by shootings.

Home sweet 'hood.

We loved entertaining, but we usually invited other starving-student friends who were also used to dodging bullets. Not penthouse-dwelling millionaires.

That night, Ron told Jeff he was taking a cab to our house because he didn't want to bring any of his cars into our neighborhood. Things were already off to a great start.

But when he arrived, he seemed fairly gracious. Charming, even, in a Daddy Warbucks kind of way. We invited him in, took his coat, then stammered for a few minutes in the entry. Embarrassed that dinner wasn't quite ready, I played a little Chopin and Brahms on the piano for him while we waited for it to come out of the oven. Then we sat down at the table, engaging him in polite conversation. Jeff offered a blessing on the food. He expressed thanks that Ron was joining us in our home for dinner.

And then it happened: Ron started to cry. As in, put his head in his hands and sobbed like a baby.

There was an awkward silence, then we asked if he was okay. He said he was fine. Wiping his eyes, he said he just couldn't get over how happy we were there. He couldn't remember ever being surrounded by so much love. We were stunned. It all seemed pretty normal to us. It's not like we put on some kind of show for this guy. And yet he sensed something unusual about the spirit in our home, and it touched him, deeply.

That evening is permanently etched in our memory. It was more than twenty years ago, before we had any kids or owned a home, before we had any money to speak of. In some ways, we didn't realize how much we had and how happy we were. But I'll always remember that it took a bald, grumpy millionaire—who had noth-ing—to point out that our life was abundantly rich.

Softening

Karen Burton

We'd lived in Los Angeles for five years—two little baby boys, no real income, and a husband who was pushing through two Master's degrees and a PhD. Not to mention a wife who usually didn't have any transportation during the day and sometimes felt a little locked in.

Don't get me wrong; we had a blast in the middle of all the stress. We made good friends that became like family, and we learned a lot about life, and struggle, and being a team. I think our marriage would be different had we not had our California years, because it was there that we learned we could do hard things. We learned that we were pretty darned independent (something this writer still pays for), and that we liked adventure.

I still find it ironic that while we lived right by the Pacific Ocean, I didn't always know the secret to helping my husband feel pacified. I blame it on being distracted with the needs of food and shelter, or even on the relatively short period we'd been together.

At times Gideon came home on the verge of breaking down under all of the pressure, like when he was close to completing his dissertation and his mentor had him rewrite large sections. That was the first time I really saw him question himself and his abilities. It was hard to watch and experience these things with him. He made the needed changes and worked hard to graduate and get on the market as soon as possible.

I realize now that I didn't thank him enough for all of his hard work and persistence during those years. He sacrificed time with the boys (especially our little guy who was born in LA) so we could get on with the business of being a family and doing family things, like getting a solid job and buying our first home. I look back now and call him our hero. Our champion.

It has been many years since we packed up a little U-Haul, said goodbye to our very best friends, and drove to BYU. We had mixed emotions about leaving a place where we'd grown so much, but at the same time, we were excited to be moving forward with a chance to see Gideon's hard work pay off.

I still see the stress show itself in my friend, my husband. He's hard on himself, knowing he has important things to do with his life. He's a visionary man in the best sense of the word. He wants to contribute all he has to make a difference in his family and his career.

Circumstances can change, but often the person deep down stays the same. The best thing about getting older is that you can see things coming from a greater distance. The signs become a little clearer, and the sharp edges of disappointment and self-doubt don't seem to cut quite so deep. I used to think it was that we got numb to things, but now I realize that it's not numbness as much as increased compassion.

That day when I first witnessed my husband having a weak moment, I was thrown. I felt tremors from uncertainty, and I had no idea how to react.

Now, after more than two decades together, I spot signals of stress much better, so I'm not blind-sided by my personal whirlwinds or ones that happen inside my home, even when they knock things off the walls. I know the Lord takes every opportunity to soften us and allow us to be less and less traumatized by life and the people in it. This isn't because we lose our sense of feeling, but because we gain more and more feeling—only now, the feeling is concern for others more than for ourselves.

Search Engines

Jana Winters Parkin

I need a search engine for my house.

Tonight I was looking for a book amid the 118 or so stacked on and around my nightstand. (Yes, I actually counted them.) I peered over dusty piles, reluctant to take them apart, just kind of giving them a sidelong glance, maybe tilting them slightly to reveal their spines for effect.

Suddenly I thought, Can't I just enter the title somewhere, and have the book I'm searching for magically appear on the top of the stack?

Google. I need Google for my overrun book collection. Now.

Then there are those elusive car keys. And the cell phone. Couldn't I just enter "keys" and "phone" when I'm ready to leave, and have Yahoo! make these essential items resurface from wherever I absent-mindedly set them . . . all by the time I get to the back door?

One night I was up until 2 AM, ransacking my office—you cannot even imagine the towers of paper I dismantled, sheet by sheet—looking for the new phone card I bought for our son. I spent untold hours searching for a card with a code that I picked up for $15. Something is very wrong with this system. I needed to be able to enter "phone card" and have it instantly materialize so I could email the code to our son. The Internet has me spoiled.

As I was pondering my need to Google things around the house (sock mate, anyone?) it occurred to me that what I really need is a search engine for my heart. Wouldn't it be great if we could summon up patience and sacrifice and forgiveness at the precise moment we need them? Separate them from all the millions of other choices swimming around inside us, and bring the top hit to the surface?

Screaming kid? Sulking teen? Husband running late? P-a-t-i-e-n-c-e (Click!) Mercy would be there, too: m-e-r-c-y (Click!). And I know that charity is buried somewhere in there, but it seems so complex. Problems arise as I keep entering incompatible searches: mercy + passive-aggression, patience + jealousy, or maybe rushed + kindness. Ultimately, it all boils down to our desires. Every good search begins with entering the right words. Sometimes we look for the wrong things because our heart's not in the right place.

I know that what I really need is something more like forgiveness + patience + mercy + generosity + compassion—but when "searching all the inward parts" the information overload threatens to crash my system. What about something simpler, like love? L-o-v-e (Click!) I need a search engine to bring charity—the purest love—to the top of the list, highlight it, and give me a link.

I'm sure that in quieter moments, the Spirit does precisely

that—works on my heart. Makes a "diligent search." Enters key words. Sorts by relevance. Brings clarity. But only when I provide the space. I need to slow down and deeply search.

From a single Source.

Lost Girl

Luisa M. Perkins

I am on a quest. I have no sword or armor. My minivan is nothing like a horse-drawn chariot. I am not even sure what I'm seeking; my only guide is an urgent sense that today, I will find something important. I go out, trusting the feeling deep in my heart that leads me to move forward like a bloodhound on a trail.

My husband Patrick, our two sons, and I are staying at The Sagamore, a posh hotel on a Lake George island in New York's Adirondack Mountains. Patrick is attending the annual conference of the U.S. Copyright Society. It is an all-expenses-paid week away from our home in Manhattan, and we are making the most of it. I have recently discovered that I have significant ancestry from the region. In fact, my great-great-great-great grandfather, John Tanner, once owned the land on which The Sagamore stands.

Genealogists in the family have assured me—somewhat smugly—that all the temple work has been done going back for centuries on the Tanner line. But today something has compelled me away from the resort's luxurious attractions and out into the countryside to nose around in search of a link to my past. I decide to visit the cemeteries in the region to see what I can see.

At Bolton Rural Cemetery, just south of the resort on Lake Shore Drive, I find the grave of John Tanner's first wife, Lydia Stewart, as well of some of their children who died in infancy. I smile, wondering about the logistics of Lydia and John's reunion on resurrection day, since John is buried some 2,000 miles away in Salt Lake City. My boys and I stroll the manicured slopes of the park-like cemetery for a while before moving on.

Federal Hill Cemetery proves almost impossible to find, its sinking, uneven grave markers obscured by tall grass. I go up and down Route 34 three times, referring to the map I purchased at the local gas station. Finally, I see what look like gravestones and stop the car. The boys can't wait to get out and explore. I push James in his stroller across the hummocky ground while Christian runs ahead, his shock of white-blond hair gleaming in the warm June sunlight. At age five, Christian has no fear of graveyards; they are places to romp while I play an obscure grown-up game I compare to hide-and-seek.

I wrangle the stroller past the headstones, examining each one as I go. Wells, French, Reynolds—these names do not interest me at the moment. But then I spy something intriguing. I kneel on the dew-soaked grass and brush the surface of the headstone lightly with my fingers. The moss and lichen splotching the granite's surface make it difficult to read, but I puzzle out the letters one by one.

Dorcas W.
Wife of Harvey D. Tanner
Died May 2, 1842
Aged 25 years 4 mos & 29 days

And next to it, a smaller stone:

Son of Harvey and Dorcas W. Tanner
Died May 2, 1842
Aged 4 years & 5 mos.

Grief washes over me—an entirely different emotion than what I've experienced at other graves. Elsewhere, I have felt a sense of homecoming, a completeness akin to sitting at Thanksgiving dinner surrounded by loved ones. But here, in this sunny, forgotten meadow, I am stricken with loss and despair.

I sit back on my haunches and ponder. What tragedy caused this mother and son to die on the same spring day so long ago? Disease? Fire? Catastrophic accident? Harvey must have been devastated; I imagine his deep anguish at losing his wife and young son in one blow.

James fidgets in his stroller, interrupting my mournful reverie. Christian runs under the tall pines at the edge of the meadow, bellowing an energetic Primary song. I should get them back to our room at the resort for their naps. I photograph both stones and transcribe the data into my notebook, and we leave.

Once home, I am glad I followed the prompting. When I check the Church's records, I find that Harvey's ordinance work was completed in the 1930s. At that time, he was sealed to his second wife, Laura Cooledge, whom he married in 1843. I also find records of their three children—the oldest of whom is named Dorcas. Another pang of vicarious grief shoots through my heart, and I applaud Laura's grace in naming her firstborn daughter after her husband's first wife.

But no matter how hard I look, there is not yet any LDS Temple record of Dorcas W. I imagine her frustration in the spirit world, blocked from progressing when her husband moved on 70 years before. Humbly, I submit her name along with young Horace's.

Later, at the Boston Temple, I complete Dorcas's work and have Horace sealed to her and Harvey. Kneeling at the altar with my husband as sacred words reunite the lost girl and her son with her husband, the joy I feel is almost indescribable. Every bit of torment that I felt kneeling by her resting place is washed away, replaced with gratitude and peace.

My quest is far from over, and can't yet (or ever) be wrapped up in a tidy bow. Discovering Dorcas's story is a work in progress; more than ten years after finding her, I still search for members of her family of origin. Hers is only one of many intriguing scraps of history I have uncovered in my genealogical digging.

I could relate other fascinating snippets—the distant cousin who worked at the U.S. Embassy in Paris and eloped with a Spanish princess; the German great-grandmother with whom I have conversed in dreams; the fallen hero whose name we discovered by chance on a monument at Omaha Beach. Each is an exciting snapshot; each is an unfinished portrait. Like an archaeologist painstakingly uncovering fossilized remains, I brush away at the layers of time that obscure the details of these lives. Slowly, the pictures come into focus; slowly, I forge real relationships with people whom I have never met.

I anticipate the day when I will encounter Dorcas in the flesh. I feel already that she is my friend. Surely we will have much to discuss—laughs to share and tears to shed. She may feel that she owes me a debt for following my heart and finding her that summer day long ago. If so, I will reply that it is I who owe her. Being a catalyst for her restoration has been one of the great blessings of my life.

"*May God bless my people, oh, remember them kindly in their time of trouble; and in the hour of their taking away.*"

James Agee

The Power of a Word:
Wherein I Uncover My Bald Spot

Becca Wilhite

I had this dumb little spot on my head, right inside my hairline over my right ear. It was scar-ish. Small-ish, pink-ish, and raised. Little. Nobody really had to see it, except when my hair was wet, which, honestly, happens every day, but usually in private moments.

One day in the fall, I came downstairs in the morning with my hair wet, and Kid 2 said, "Ewww. What's up with that thing on your head?"

To which I responded, "None of your business. Eat your breakfast." But then, of course, everyone wanted to see my little scar. Which, apparently was growing larger, as opposed to following the growing-smaller plan I had for it.

I'm afraid this might be a long story; feel free to skip to the end. Or grab a handful of pistachios. Or declaw the cat. Whatever.

When my husband took a good look at it, he said, "You're calling somebody."

I tried to placate him. "It's nothing."

His eyes widened as he poked at me. "Bec, it's growing," he said, in that voice that oozes concern. As though the little scar was going to take over my face or something.

"Yeah, okay. I'll call." Which, by the way, I did, after only a few days and some email-style prodding.

A few weeks later, I went to the dermatologist. Nice guy—if you like your doctors efficient and businesslike, which I do. He said, "Oh, hey, we see things weirder than this every day. The sun probably just damaged your skin because you spent a Whole Lot of Years in the sun. A whole lot. Let's just scrape it off."

So I got biopsied. Cute Megan the nurse/assistant told me I'd feel a little prick (that was for the numbing shot). I squeezed my fingers together waiting for it. I think I might have even been holding my breath, waiting for that little prick, when Cute Megan said, "Okay, all done. Keep this lubed with this greasy Polysporin gunk."

(Or she may have said something possibly slightly more science-y. You get the point.)

They shuffled me out the door saying, "Yadda, yadda, thanks, we'll call you if it's anything, blah, blah, keep it moist, whatever."

A week later, I got the weirdest phone call. "Hi, Becca," the nurse who was not Cute Megan said, "We just wanted to call you because we got your biopsy back, and it's skin cancer." She kept talking.

I heard words, but they didn't mean anything. It was one of those moments when the time continuum sort of opens up, and you think, right there in that space between syllables, Huh. Cancer. That really, really stinks.

I felt hollow in my brain and in my guts. I let her calm voice and her words wash over me, and I started hearing things like "a million people a year," and, "really simple," and "not dangerous," and "basal cell," and "carcinoma," and "removed," and I reminded myself to breathe.

Then I sat down on the floor and didn't get up for a long time.

I have cancer. I have cancer? Are you kidding me?

Apparently not.

And then, into my head:

Remember the sunblock you don't wear? You have no right, no right at all to mourn this news. You deserve this because you worship the sun. You are like the chain smoker who moans about lung cancer. You are the worst kind of lame. You may not feel sad, only guilty. And not only that—it isn't even real cancer (that word again, oh, that word makes my guts sick.) because you don't have to have treatments. You just go in and they cut out the spot, and they stitch you up, and you drive yourself home and you go back in six months (forever) and over and over you face the full-body-scan humiliation and the doctor will keep taking spots off your skin, and you'll be grateful that it isn't on the end of your nose. Yet.

And then:

Not only that, but you really can't play in the sun anymore. You can't make it worse than it already is. Who cares that you have stupid sensitive skin that reacts with welts and hives when you wear sunblock? Nobody, that's who. The tan portion of your life is over. Learn to love white fat. Yes, brown fat is prettier. Deal with it.

And then:

Oh. Cancer. That word is so big and powerful for a collection of just a few letters. None of the letters are even tall. But the word—it takes a bite out of your soul, doesn't it? It makes you sink to the floor and stay there. It gives you visions of your very own body, the body you have never loved enough, fighting against itself for cellular domination. Cancer is a word that brings its own bags and moves in and lives on your couch and never, ever goes away.

And then I held my knees and said, just in my head, I have cancer.

After that, I tried it out loud. "I have cancer." I said it three times. Each time, it pinched my mouth. It tasted like charcoal dust.

Then I breathed for a few minutes.

I called my husband. And do you know what happened when I made that call? I turned into The Protector. Does this happen to you? I decided who absolutely had to know (only my husband at that point), and I told the story with as much cushioning as I could manage. It started with the demand that he not worry. Because this was not a big deal. I wonder now—did I mean that at all? I echoed the nice nurse's words about a million people a year, and basal cells, and ease. I mentioned the part about driving myself home (a big deal, because I'd made an appointment for the next day, when my husband was locked into a film shoot that he couldn't miss). I probed for fear, for concern, for worry, and I swept them all away with the power of my words.

But underneath, there was the other word. The heavy word. The one that tried to pull all my cushy comfort words down and drown them.

I decided to tell the parents. Again with the cushioning. Again with the careful protecting. Again with the making sure that they were all fine. And then I asked them for prayers. That this small thing not turn into a big thing. Which prayers they promised. And I felt.

And for the rest of the day, I sat. I thought. I allowed myself the day to mourn. To grieve. To let go forever the thought of my mortal immortality. To set aside my delusion of wholeness. I asked myself for forgiveness.

The next day, I went and had the spot removed (which was weird, because after the biopsy, it was pretty much gone). My stepmama came with me. She held my eyes with hers so I could try to miss the scissors and the needles and the no-longer-white gauze that danced around my periphery. I asked a few questions. I laughed with the doctor (or maybe it was only me laughing) and with Cute Megan the nurse. I tried to pretend that I couldn't hear the scissoring, but who was I kidding? There was that unfortunate nicking of the temporal artery and the subsequent mess. I walked out with a pressure bandage that stuck out of my head a whole inch, but could be covered by hair much thicker than mine. I carried on.

And inside, there was that word. Oh, that word. Cancer. It still sits there, heavy in my brain (metaphorically, okay? this is still about "just" basal cell carcinoma), and I carry it everywhere. There are days when the weight of that word makes writing hard. There are days when I want to say to all my demands, Hey, don't you know that there's cancer in here? But I can't. Because, remember? It's the "just" kind. The kind that isn't dangerous. The kind that I brought on myself. The kind that is so much more an emotional cancer than a physical one. I think that is the final balance-tipping piece.

I would allow myself to mourn more, to grieve more, if the physical were as big as it could be—if there was a treatment, or a medication, or horrible chemo in my future. But since there's not— "just" an occasional bald spot from lesion-removal—I feel like I've had my moment to mourn, and now I have to get back in the saddle.

It has been a sad thing. Sadness, it gets in the way, sometimes. But not every time. And carrying on is what we do. We who are strong and weak, and we who are whole and damaged, and we who are powerful and frail, and we who are fearless and daunted. We carry on.

We pray.

We listen.

We learn.

We feel.

We forgive and seek forgiveness.

We carry on.

And some of us seek to channel the power of other powerful words.

The healing kind.

We Are Clear Blocks of Ice

Karen Burton

Every year since 1989, in the most northern reaches of Sweden, 200 kilometers (about 124 miles) above the Arctic Circle, artists and architects get together to build a giant hotel made exclusively of ice. Three thousand tons of ice, in the form of huge blocks, are cut out of the local Torne River and stored in a huge warehouse. They're kept there from March – when they are cut out of the river – until November. The construction takes three weeks.

The hotel is not only loaded with room after room for guests, but it houses a soaring, domed chapel supported by 20-foot columns. Each room is monochromatically luminous with its ice sculptures and ice furniture, and fiber optics are strung through thousands of square feet to add to the magical feeling. It's an amazing thing to behold, even though I've only seen it on television and in photos.

But the most amazing thing of all is the disappearance of the entire structure within three months, when it finally melts into the ground from whence it came. From the minute of its completion, the hotel starts to change. Even the breath of the visitors subtly thaws walls and ceilings and art. It's a living thing, and it begins its death immediately, not unlike us.

Beautifully made, with detail and care, we shine and display our own art. As we welcome guests into our lives, we change, through their presence, until our time comes to melt back into our starting place, gorgeous and flowing, like a clear river.

The Last Day

Becca Wilhite

Standing at the circulation desk, filing cards grown soft at the corners, I heard the phone ring. Eager for a change of pace, even if it meant I'd be doing someone's research over the phone, I grabbed the receiver.

"Batesville Public Library, can I help you?"

It was my dad, calling from a hospital room in Chicago, where my mom had been admitted during their getaway weekend. He just wanted to check in on me—he'd missed me when he called home to talk to the boys.

"I'm good. Work is fine. I'm excited to go to Cincinnati this afternoon. Can I talk to Mom?"

Pause.

Now, I should explain that pauses in telephone conversations with my dad are not unusual. There is always . . . a great deal . . . of

. . . white space . . . in talking with him.

So why was I suddenly hot around my eyes, and tight in the back of my throat?

"Dad?"

Throat-clearing. "No. You can't. Mom's in a coma."

Did I know that? Was there some conversation in the past few days where this information was given to me, and did I somehow forget about it? Is that even possible? But if not, how could he have neglected to mention such a vital fact to me?

The library, quiet anyway, went fuzzy like cotton around me. Even the whispers were muffled, and I felt wrapped up in the familiar. I didn't even sit down. I tipped my chin to roll the tears back into my head, and I finished the conversation like a well-bred teenager. Which I was.

Maybe years of living with a mom who spent a week every year in the hospital had calloused me. Maybe the idea of her in the ICU was just part of my childhood. I'd lived with it my whole life, you know. So maybe you won't find me a completely unfeeling ingrate when I tell you that the rest of the day was more than fine—it was fun.

After a rowdy drive into Cincinnati, Missy and I got dropped off downtown, scoured a few ballet supply stores (for her) and a bookstore (for me). We ate at Taco Bell. For a skinny person, Missy could really eat. She ordered no fewer than five menu items, and I watched, impressed, as she downed every bite. We met at the rendezvous point to get picked up for the dance.

The dance.

Here was where I belonged, in this under-decorated church-building-turned-social-hall. With these kids, from towns and cities an hour from my home—this was where I felt like me. Good kids, and all so different. Different from what I saw every day at school, and different from each other. I felt loved there, not judged, not watched, not weird. This was a place for a great deal of hugging.

Dance, dance, dance. Cute boys and happy girls and jokes and laughter and music. Forgive me for forgetting, for a couple of hours, what was going on a few hundred miles to the northwest.

After the dance, Pizza. As ever. Mr. G's pizza, breadsticks, and root beer. More laughing. More talk. More teasing. Gentle teasing from the others, and more pointed teasing from my brother. I shook it off, like I'd learned to do (not like the years and years before, when I would scream and yell and then get in trouble for overreacting).

Somehow on the long drive home, I didn't know. I had no premonitions. The earth didn't shift. Air wasn't sucked from the atmosphere. I just rode home, laughing and not sleepy and not afraid.

I checked on my little brother. He was sleeping in the parent's big bed, elbows and knees everywhere. Good. Wash face. Brush teeth. Change into jammies. Lights off. Climb into bed.

Knock at the door.

Blood runs cold.

Ignore it. It will go away. My fear of the dark, fueled by far too many Stephen King novels that first year I worked at the library, overtook all logic.

More knocking.

Monsters. Axe murderers. Doorbell. Vampires. Psychotic animals.

More knocking. Another doorbell.

I picked up the phone in my room and called our own number.

I don't know if this works anymore, technologically speaking, but that night, I hung up quickly, and the phone began to ring. Once, twice, three times. It stopped. I grabbed the receiver.

"Hello?" My big brother pretended not to be asleep.

"It's me."

"What?"

"There's someone at the door."

Only the intervention of a benevolent God prevented him from reminding me that axe murderers do not ring doorbells.

"Okay. Coming." The bravest words of a brave big brother.

I stood, shivering at my bedroom door. Saw him walk from the basement stairs across the small family room. He turned and I heard the door open. Heard the grownups' voices, hushed appropriately for the time of night and the delicacy of their mission.

I didn't wonder if we'd left something in their car. I didn't wonder if anything terrible had happened to their kids between dropping us off and getting themselves home. I didn't wonder anything.

Because I knew.

I knew.

I walked to the front door. They'd come inside, but only just. Their backs were pressed against the door, and I knew again. There were no jokes, and if these two weren't telling jokes, this was more serious than anything I'd ever experienced with them. Jolene, tall and stricken, held her arms out to me. I shook my head, not because I didn't want her comfort, not because I didn't believe, but because my head would shake. Back and forth as I was folded into her arms.

Whispered words: "Your mom . . ."

Head shake, back and forth.

". . . dad called . . . "

Head shake.

"Come home with us, sleep at our house . . . "

And then I could nod. Yes. Your house. That is the right thing to do. Because we shouldn't be here alone. And we should give you the thing you need, too. We should allow you to do the only thing to do when there is nothing, nothing anyone can do.

Before getting in the car, I did the only thing I could do when there was nothing else to do: I went back into my room, picked up the phone again, and listened as the buttons sang her song—the eleven-note jingle that meant I could reconnect with my far-far-away best friend.

Her mom told me she was asleep.

"Please. I need her. My mom died."

Gasp. "Oh, Becca." A quick waking, and there it was. The comfort I needed, across a thousand miles. The words, just right.

Will you be shocked, or will you understand when I tell you we laughed? Will you know what it is to share a heart, to realize that there is a time for tears, and a time for laughter? And, sometimes, will you understand the need for both at once? Will you know that both, in equal measure, are required to heal?

Fathers: Shaping Life and Death

Jana Winters Parkin

L ike many of us, my most salient memories of fathers have to do
with giving birth. But mine also have to do with facing death.
One memory is filled with surprise and delight. The other is poi-
gnantly heartbreaking. Both swim rapturously in love and admiration.

* * *

My mom was slowly dying while I was expecting our first
child. We shared so much throughout that pregnancy. We were both
violently ill—she with cancer and chemotherapy, and I with morning sickness that lasted all day, the entire nine months. Mom and I
talked every day, laughing and commiserating as we compared notes
on who threw up more, who ached the most, and marveling at the
similarities between birthing and dying.

She was present at the birth of our son, a miracle for both of
us. Mom was right there in the delivery room, feeding me ice chips,

placing cool rags on my forehead, and literally breathing with me through the contractions. My dad was there too—I think mostly to be with her.

Mom died six months after Josh was born. One of my last memories of her is watching her kiss him from her hospital bed—a few moments of joy in a very long ordeal.

I also remember stepping from her hospital room into the hall-way with my dad, and catching sight of my white-haired 87-year-old grandpa making his way down the hall, dressed in a suit. This look of total relief came over my dad, and tears came to his eyes.

"That's my dad," he tried to explain. "After all these years, I still need him; he's my hero."

When I became pregnant with our second child, a daughter, I missed my mom like never before. The nausea and vomiting seemed so much worse because I was suffering through it alone. I couldn't call my mom and commiserate. And I couldn't imagine delivering another baby without her there. (Although I frequently dreamed about her during the most trying times.) The pregnancy seemed endless. In fact, it kind of was. She was sixteen days late.

My water broke around midnight. Knowing the delivery lasted 23 1/2 hours with our firstborn, I didn't bother calling anyone in the middle of the night to let them know I was in labor . . . there was still plenty of time for that. The doctor said to wait until I was "really uncomfortable" before we went to the hospital, so I hung out at home, doubling over the kitchen counter when the contractions got fierce.

All of a sudden, around 2 a.m. I declared that I was, indeed, "really uncomfortable" and we went to the hospital. When they checked me in, I was already dilated to an eight. They gave me an epidural to help me sleep—and I think mostly so the doctor wouldn't have to come and deliver in the middle of the night.

Our little daughter popped out in just two pushes the next morning. It was almost as if someone had swooped down from heaven and placed her in my arms. We called our families to announce that we had a girl, then they wheeled her off to the nursery—and me to the recovery room, where I settled in for a long winter's nap. Jeff went home to gather a few things, and as I was just waking up, still a little groggy, I heard the hospital room door creak open. I slowly turned to see who it was, and there stood my dad.

He said he knew where my mom was going to be this morning, and he wanted to be there too.

I have no idea how he managed to get there so fast, how many people he had to pay off at the airport to get on the first flight out of town, but at a time when I was missing Mom and feeling very much alone, to have my dad magically appear at the hospital was about my favorite surprise ever.

"That's my dad," I wanted to say. "After all these years, I still need him. He's my hero."

* * *

In October of 2000, my husband, Jeff, was away for the long weekend, picking up some heirloom furniture for our daughter's room. I was home with the kids, nearly six months pregnant with baby number four, unpacking boxes in the new dream house. When I first noticed the baby wasn't moving, I phoned him immediately. I tried to reassure him: "The book says it's normal not to feel any movement at this stage," but I could hear the deep concern in his voice. At his insistence, I called the doctor and ordered a follow-up ultrasound. Just to be safe.

My husband was late for the ultrasound appointment, so I sat there—alone—as the doctor searched for a heartbeat, and found none. I also sat by myself—in horror—as he explained to me the options for delivering a lifeless baby. They asked me to wait, alone (in tears that bordered on convulsions) in a room that was more like a closet—until Jeff arrived, forty minutes later. Then I had to sit through the whole painful doctor spiel a second time, for Jeff.

As we walked into the hospital delivery room a day and a half later, I struggled with all kinds of emotions that kept bubbling to the surface. It was strange to walk into the familiar maternity ward that had, until that moment, been such a happy place and which now wore a shroud of gloom for me, knowing that this time there would be no treasure to take home. I fought back feelings of anger and resentment toward my sweet, wonderful husband for being away when I threatened miscarriage and had to go to the emergency room passing clots, being away when the baby stopped moving, being away when the doctor delivered the unthinkable news. Part of me wanted to push him away forever, but a stronger part wanted to pull him infinitely closer. My steps were heavy, and my heart was heavier

Once we were settled inside the delivery room, Jeff gave me a beautiful priesthood blessing. He summoned our Father and poured out peace, requested health and healing, assured me that my mother would be hovering nearby, and promised a deepened understanding of how it pained a Father to lose a Child. I recognized that all good fathers live a pattern of caring and support that emulates our Heavenly Father: compassionately shepherding us through life's deepest sorrows and greatest joys.

The delivery was a physical and emotional hell, like nothing I've experienced before or since. The only things that could calm me, emotionally or physically, were Rachmaninov's Second Piano Concerto and the memory of Jeff's blessing. Somehow I stopped shaking and survived.

After the baby was born, so small I could cushion her whole head in the pillow of my palm (I still recall the weight of it there), they made prints of both her hands and her feet, and allowed me to hold her and cradle her and look at her and love her for as long as I liked. I touched each tiny finger, each tiny toe, and marveled at how complete she was, despite weighing less than a pound. She had our youngest's perfect little button nose. Our other daughter's beautiful rosebud lips. There was no doubt she was ours. She belonged to us. But she'd already gone home.

When the nurse came to take her away, Jeff was holding her. I watched as he wrapped her so lovingly in her little blanket and said his last goodbyes. He kissed her tiny forehead and handed her to the nurse. I cannot describe the rush of love that I felt for that man at that moment. It was overwhelming to witness the immense tenderness he demonstrated for our little departed daughter. His sweet, intimate farewell to her is among the most priceless images I carry. I felt unspeakably grateful for him and his enormous heart.

Miscarriage

Ken Craig

By the last week of April, our plans for a November baby were in place, and anticipation was settling in.

By the first week in May, we knew a miscarriage was imminent.

It didn't sneak up on us, but I'm not sure how you prepare for something like that. Katie had known something was wrong for a few days, and she was grappling with the possibility of a miscarriage long before I considered it. Even though she told me her concerns, I dismissed them. I didn't discount that something might be wrong, or insist that it wouldn't be a miscarriage. But I held on to the thought—or, maybe hope—that it was something else. Something less definite.

I don't think I realized how much of that day for Katie was spent processing what was most likely happening, or what could be happening, or what she hoped wasn't happening. As her husband, without the constant reminder that life is growing within me, I operated on the daily assumption that when Katie didn't tell me anything, it meant that everything was fine, and when she did tell me something, I could take a moment to wish and hope it away.

I prayed often for Katie. More than morning and night. But I remember the palpable moment I realized that my prayers and supplications were subconsciously, or maybe intuitively, always for Katie, not necessarily for the baby. That's when I started slowly, quietly, to accept what was already impressing upon me in small waves.

This baby was not coming.

Over the next few days, we didn't discuss it much. I didn't understand what might be happening, so I didn't know what to prepare for. I often hugged her and asked, "Are you okay?"

She looked away, distracted, dealing with her own feelings. "Yes," she said simply, and moved on with her tasks.

It seemed so ineffectual, merely asking if she was okay. I wished I could tell her what was really in my heart. I wanted to say, "I'm so sorry this is happening to you. I'm so sorry I can only stand here, completely helpless, and watch you emotionally drawn and quartered. I'm sorry I don't know how to make this all go away and heal your body and strengthen your soul. Please tell me what I can do to show my concern. Please tell me that you're not okay, but that if I were to do this or that, you would be. And please, please don't let me go through this by myself."

Then, late one evening, Katie asked me for a priesthood blessing. I knew the request was time-sensitive, so I immediately called a close friend and asked him to assist me in administering to my wife. As I placed my hands on Katie's head, I felt how loved she was by her Father in Heaven. How known she was. How important.

I waited for the clarity to come that all would be well with the baby, but it wasn't happening. I waited longer. Never had I struggled more against the impulse to mix my emotions with revelation on someone's behalf. Everything in me wanted to tell Katie that she'd be blessed to give birth to a beautiful baby and that her body would heal. That life would be as wonderful as she hoped.

But those impressions never arrived. I found myself making all kinds of promises to my Heavenly Father, if only He would grant us this one blessing. But I knew what needed to be said. I felt impressed to promise Katie that this experience would draw her closer to Him, that whether a baby came or not, she would be at peace in her heart and mind, and in her soul. Somehow, that knowledge brought me a degree of hope I hadn't anticipated.

The next morning, Katie seemed remarkably calm. Not carefree, but peaceful. She said she knew this pregnancy wouldn't develop into a child. And she been calmed and comforted by the priesthood blessing. I could see that she had been blessed with understanding and insight. I felt reassured by her confidence. My feelings up to that morning had been focused on Katie's well-being. A miscarriage would affect her physically as well as emotionally and mentally. My understanding and acceptance of what was happening were a direct response to hers; I was relieved at her confidence and was now determined that everything would be fine. If Katie was at peace, so was I.

Right?

Wrong.

I left for work that morning, hoping that the background noise of the radio would provide a needed distraction during my commute. I was ten minutes into my drive when the world suddenly slowed down and my mind became singularly focused.

I began to process my own reaction to the reality that a child I was eager to know and love would not be arriving. I felt like I was going to miss the chance to meet somebody who would have affected my life in a beautiful way . . . and there was no way to retrieve that specific opportunity. Suddenly I felt swallowed up in sadness. I wasn't angry or resentful. I didn't feel cheated or that life was unfair. I just felt sad. And that sadness enveloped me.

The radio became hushed, so I just turned it off. I became unaware of other cars, other drivers. The air was still and stifling, and I felt energy draining off me like steam. When I arrived at the office, I pulled into the parking lot and sat in my car, with no initiative to leave my seat.

Typically, my emotions are very near the surface under even the most benign circumstances; so with the profound sadness, I found myself crying, quietly. I wasn't overwhelmed with emotion, nor did I feel that my exterior was cracking. But I knew I didn't feel like talking about what was going on.

I worked half the day and then left for an ultrasound appointment with our midwife. As Katie and I drove to the office, our conversation included speculations from one side of the spectrum to the other. From "Maybe I was never pregnant," to "What if we're completely off and everything is okay?" But when the ultrasound showed what we had already suspected—that a miscarriage was imminent—we weren't surprised.

Sadness briefly stung my heart again, and I studied Katie's face, searching for any detectable sorrow. I thought I could see it, but it was buried under a brave, accepting demeanor, so I didn't say a word. I felt like speaking would have pulled the foundational block out from under her pyramid of strength, and her calm exterior might have given way. And that just seemed unnecessary. So I simply squeezed her hand.

We drove home somewhat oddly comforted in knowing for certain where we were at physically. We didn't say anything to anybody else, as we hadn't told anybody about the pregnancy, not even our parents. The next couple of days were spent watching and waiting, but they brought us closer. I felt conscious of Katie and what was going on inside her.

At the end of that week, my parents were set to arrive at our house for the weekend, and literally, as I heard my kids squealing that Grandma and Grandpa were here, Katie found me and told me that it had just happened. She cried a light, heartfelt sigh of relief, finally feeling that she had turned a page and felt closure from a long, uncertain experience. I hugged her so close, I wasn't sure if I was sustaining her or she, me.

I walked outside and met my parents at their car. I hugged them, helped grab their stuff, and then told them a little about what the last week had been like. I wanted to let them know so they could be sensitive to Katie.

My dad and I were taking my boys camping for the night, and Katie, my mom and the girls had planned a girls' night at home. As Katie went into the kitchen to start their special dinner, my mom pulled Katie in to her and said, "Don't you worry about dinner. We're going out. Let's take it easy tonight."

I watched Katie melt into my mom's embrace, crying. Of

course it was more than the promise that she wouldn't have to cook dinner. It was being understood, being cared for. It was the profound link between women, between mothers. It was an answer to prayer and the fulfillment of a blessing. My mom had had a miscarriage between my two youngest brothers, so she understood much more deeply than I did—though I wanted to. Katie felt her understanding. I'll always be grateful that my mom was there; that she is exactly who she is, with the instincts that she has, with the love she's had for Katie since day one.

Later, as I thought about that moment, I realized how many people I know and love who have had miscarriages. For how common they are, rarely are they discussed. I imagine it's because the event may be common, but the experience is personal. It was for us. It seems like a private grieving—mourning the loss of possibilities, of plans.

We have since added a seventh child to our little family. Like her brothers and sisters, she has brought with her a measure of joy to our lives that goes beyond expression. We're grateful for her sweet spirit in our home.

I'll always remember that touch of sadness that accompanied the unique experience of what might have been. But through it all, I knew Heavenly Father was mindful of us, that he was aware of our anxiety, our sorrow. And I know He is aware of our unwavering gratitude for the blessing of family.

'Children are an heritage of the Lord,' the Psalmist writes.

I couldn't agree more.

Letting Daddy Die

Debbie Frampton

He is face down on the floor, hair carefully combed, arms folded tightly under his chest. His favorite red flannel shirt is tucked neatly into his dark denim jeans and thick brown belt for special occasions. Directly above him on the floor is a framed portrait of Christ smiling serenely, a lamb across his shoulders. On his right side, where his face is tilted, is a photograph of us—all of us—taken at a scout fundraiser just before the separation. In it his grin is far too wide.

"Look happy!" he'd said through clenched teeth, then, BAM, we all said "cheese," and it was done.

My sister enters the room behind me, and my mom is still climbing the front porch stairs. We don't see her come in; we only hear her telling my dad we brought him some homemade bread before her voice snags in her throat.

A moment of silence. A pause before the pain.

My sister leans forward, bends her knees, and, as if yanked out of thin air, is caught in my mind like a fish on a hook, flopping on the couch beside the body. My mom kneels down and places two fingers over his neck. She freezes, covers her mouth and, eyes wide, twists her neck backwards. Now she is trotting from the body to the phone and to the open window where the sun shoots into the room, exposing my dad in various shades of death.

The March air bites into my skin, and I begin to shake. Spring has sprung like a mousetrap.

Across the street, a postman strides into view, nodding pleasantly at a woman pushing a stroller. The postman says something to the baby, which makes the woman smile. A toddler, trailing behind, sprinkles Cheerios from a baggie into the leftover crusted snow, where a flock of birds gather and peck incessantly. When the Cheerios are gone, the toddler begins to point and scream, and then three firemen burst into the room. One of them has his arm around my mom. She looks at him with large, glassy eyes, and he directs her to the couch.

"Looks like he's already gone," says one fireman to another.

The toddler continues to scream across the street. His mom points and tells him, "Lookie! Fire truck!" But it's no use.

My mom is sitting on the couch now and nodding. Now she's lying down, and the fireman is telling her that everything is going to be all right, but she keeps popping up like a Weeble.

"Ma'am, can I ask when you last saw your husband?" he asks.

"Yesterday," she tells him.

I didn't see him yesterday. I could have, but I didn't, because there was a school dance. I can't remember the last time I saw him, actually. Was it The Beach Boys concert when he got tripped out and drove way too fast on the way home?

"See ya later, alligator," he'd said when he dropped me off, his voice vague and muffled as if he was chewing cotton balls.

Had I seen him later? I couldn't remember. There was the time in the school cafeteria when I ran for class secretary and pretended not to notice him putting up campaign posters for me. There was the night he walked me home from his apartment after I came to borrow $10. "You don't have to walk me home," I told him, but he insisted. He tried to ask me about boys and school, but I just rolled my eyes. He told me about a great book written by a young girl named Anne Frank.

"You should read that book," he said.

"I have," I told him.

The toddler's screams get louder and louder and then stop suddenly in front of the house.

Two medics burst into the room with a stretcher. They turn the body over, and I look away. When I look back, Dad is hooked up. There's a whir of buzzing and ringing, followed by a few broken beeps, and then they pull out flat metal paddles and rub them together. I look away again. They're going to jumpstart him. I exhale. That's all he needs . . . just one more jump. Turn the ignition, and his motor will ignite. I am sure of it. And then his coloring will return to normal.

In three days, it will be April first, and I'll feel the same surety as his casket is lowered into the ground. I'll hold my breath, positive that he'll bust out with his wide grin and shout "April fools!"

DEBBIE FRAMPTON

It made sense. The ultimate practical joke from the ultimate practical joker. He'd pulled off a real hum dinger. You got me, Dad, I'd say. For a second there, you were nearly dead.

No, he would correct me, for a second there I was nearly alive. When I look back, the stretcher is in mid-air, suspended for a moment between here and there as my dad passes me in a blur of stinging red and violet.

"Tell me," I ask my sister later, "was the toddler still crying when they lifted him into the ambulance?"

"No," she says. "There was no toddler."

"What about the body? What was it like when you found him?"

"He was face down," she says, "lying on his stomach. His arms were tucked up underneath him, and the window was open. He was wearing his favorite red flannel shirt . . . and jeans, I think." At this point she begins to blink back tears. "The thing is . . ." she says, "There was this picture of Christ on the floor above him. And there was that family photo . . ." Her voice trails off.

"The one we had taken for that scout fund raiser?" I finish.

"Yes, that one . . . "

I could have been there, I almost tell her.

I would have been . . .

"Just be happy you weren't there," she tells me.

But I should have been. I still find him there sometimes, lying on the floor, his hair carefully combed and his red flannel shirt neatly tucked into his jeans. Sometimes I get there before he dies. I close the window and cover him with a blanket. He cries a little and says God forgive me as his breathing gets louder and raspier. He gasps when he realizes that he's really done it this time. He wants to change his mind, make things right, but it's too late. His chest is already heaving.

Other times, I get there before he puts the needle in. I sit next to him on the floor and see his tears. Daddy, are you okay? I say. I reach out and put my hand on his shoulder. Do you need to talk?

He opens his eyes with surprise. Don't worry about me, honey, he tells me, but I stay and wait.

Later he asks, why are you here anyway? Do you need something?

No, I tell him. I just came to see if you were okay.

Sometimes I ask him to recall our last memory together. This is our last memory together, he says.

No, for real, I say.

He pauses and smiles. You? For real?

Eventually he always breaks down and tells me that he couldn't take it anymore. That he was a failure . . . a sinner. He tells me he messed everything up. He buries his face in his hands and apologizes for being such a disappointment to me. I know you're ashamed of me, he says. He tells me that he's ashamed of himself. He's sorry about all the times he shot up while we were around and how he wished I hadn't seen him that way—how he wished my friends hadn't seen him that way. And finally he says that he's sick, and he's sick of being sick.

You'll all be better off without me.

I rub his shoulders and tell him I'm sorry too, and that everything will be okay, that I understand he's having a rough go of it and I know he's trying his best. I love you, daddy, I tell him.

It's a lie, but later it will become the truth.

He sits up and hugs me and says, You don't really mean that.

Of course I mean it, I say, even though I don't, yet.

I skip the school dance that night and make popcorn, and we watch some TV together. We talk about boys and school and the *Diary of Anne Frank*, and I thank him for the campaign posters. He gives me butterfly kisses before my wedding and a high five when I graduate college.

But usually, after all of our talking and crying and hugging, he puts the needle in anyway, and the medics carry him out.

After a while, crocodile, he says as he passes me standing in his living room.

Wait! I call out, and the medics stop. I said I was sorry!

Shhh. He puts his finger to his lips. It's not that simple.

Well, I'm not just going to stand here and let you die! I call after him.

You already have, he calls back. Then poof, he disappears.

Sing me to Sleep

Jana Winters Parkin

My mother was a singer, a pianist, and a conductor. I always think of her as the most joyful and alive when she was directing a chorus. Music was her life. And her life-blood. We were so privileged to grow up in a home where:

- Late at night we'd drift off to sleep listening to the muffled notes of Beethoven's "Pathetique" sonata ringing out from the grand piano upstairs.
- On Tuesdays, we'd come home from school to a live chamber music session (piano, cello, and flute) passionately rehearsing in the living room.
- After Christmas dinner she'd tune all the crystal goblets to a perfect scale, and we'd play carols by running our fingers over the rims.
- We'd move the couches and have an impromptu polka party, just for fun, with her at the piano.

- We learned to sing "Tender Shepherd" as a round before we could even talk.
- We gathered around the piano and sang hymns in four-part harmony before going to bed.

So it was only appropriate that when the cancer had finally consumed her body and the cheynes-stokes breathing indicated that she was not long for this earth, we reached for hymn books. Now it was our turn to sing her to sleep.

The grief counselor told us that hearing is the last thing to go. So even when it doesn't look like a loved one is paying attention, when they no longer have the strength to respond, and might even appear to be unconscious, they can still listen.

We each took a moment to say our goodbyes. And then we started to sing. At first it was hesitant, awkward. We fumbled for parts as we choked back tears. Gradually, flipping through the hymn book to find our favorites, the most comforting ones, we gained confidence. Our voices rang out in a rich blend. My sweet brother Ben climbed right up onto her bed and lay next to Mom, crooning softly into her ear with his golden voice.

Then, amazingly, our sound was somehow amplified, as though we were joined by a growing chorus of angels. As we sang "I Need Thee Every Hour," we were so caught up in the moment, the richness of the music, the power of the performance, we almost didn't notice . . . then someone pointed us back to reality, and we watched in awe: on the last phrase of the last verse, right when we sang, "O bless me now, my Savior, I come to thee," Mom took her last breath.

And I felt the veil part, as though the very divider between heaven and earth slipped open just a crack, to let her soul pass through. In that instant, so full-to-the-brim it couldn't be stopped, some light and truth and love seeped through from the other side. It filled the room and wrapped around us, bathing us in its warmth.

I remember feeling so beautiful inside that I wanted to hang onto that moment forever and ever. I have never been so sure in all my life of the reality of an after-life; that my mother's soul slipped away to someplace bigger and better than we could possibly imagine. That she was with God.

I never imagined that her moment of death would have such a lasting impact on me. That over all the years of teaching and training and loving and serving and, yes, laughing, that what I would remember best was her leaving—and the amazing cushion of peace she left behind. She told me once she wanted to be remembered as a peacemaker. And now she is.

I love that—just once—when it mattered most, I got to sing my mother to sleep.

Orphan

Melanie Jacobson

No one expects to be an orphan. Assuming your first lucid memory isn't the Dickensian walls of an actual orphanage, most of us figure we're going to have our parents long enough to watch them bouncing our children on their knees.

But I was orphaned at the age of thirty-two. One day I had both of my parents. And then two months later, I didn't.

We knew that the return of my mom's breast cancer meant her jig was up, but my dad's death first shocked us. A flu layered on top of a few other things did him in, and suddenly my wedding to the man of my dreams was bookended by the funerals of my parents by a month on either side.

And then I was an orphan.

Orphan.

I roll that word around in my mouth sometimes. If I say it out loud, it sounds maudlin, as if I should hear the sad strains of organ music in the background. As a culture, we don't use it much anymore. We save it for kids adopted out of China or former Eastern Bloc countries. Or for movie children dressed in itchy-looking wool, pre-1940.

Maybe the term fell out of favor when orphanages morphed into "group homes," or when the foster system grew. But whether the term is fashionable or not, I am one: an orphan.

An orphan with a husband and three kids, a minivan and a solidly middle-class house, a carpool, and a standing girls' night out with other suburban moms, to be sure. But I'm still an orphan. And oddly, the romanticized orphan experiences we see in Oliver Twist and Annie aren't far off the mark.

Like those apple-cheeked kiddos, I dream about finding a mother. I look for her everywhere. Maybe I'll be assigned a kindly widow to visit teach, and she will adopt me, I think. I drift into that daydream sometimes during Relief Society, where I study the faces of the over-sixty set and wonder which one would like to step up and take care of me.

I'm nearing forty, and I had a solid three decades with my own mom, so you'd think it wouldn't matter. I thought it wouldn't. As I watched her slip toward death, I thought, I can do this. I can move forward without her here every day. I am fully formed. I'm marrying a good man. We'll have a good partnership. I'm not alone."

And I'm not.

But I'm motherless, and that's a hard thing to be when I have three small faces looking up at me, daily demanding the thousand things that children legitimately need, like love and affection and Lego time on the floor with me. When I am trying to figure out how to comfort one and feed the others and help each child feel seen and loved, I know I'm failing because there's not enough of me to do it all.

That's when a mother knows to say, "They know you love them. Right now, it's enough. You're a good mom." More than anyone else, I need to hear those words from the person who taught me everything I know about mothering.

I miss my dad, of course. I'd like to pick his brain sometimes about how to better shape my oldest son's study habits, or how to prepare him to hold the priesthood. When I had the important men in my son's life write him letters of advice and guidance for his twelfth birthday, I ached at the absence of words from my dad. But I'm sure that my children have a wonderful father. I'm far less sure that they have a wonderful mother. And that's why I specifically miss my mom in the hard parenting moments.

I think that maybe if she were still here, she could make up for my deficiencies, fill in the gaps where I fail to be the nurturer I should be. I want her to step in until I pull myself together enough to handle it.

I think I'm supposed to take comfort in the notion of "someday." That's what the gospel teaches us, isn't it? That someday we'll be together and then my mother will embrace me and point to my children who are grown with children of their own. They'll surround us in the nebulous forever of eternity, and then she will say, "They're all here. You're a good mom."

So there's always someday. But that doesn't help me now.

Now is hard. Now is when I am uncertain of what to do when my children flatly refuse to eat the foods that will make them grow strong and healthy. Now is when I am a total hypocrite as I pray over the nightly chicken nuggets to "nourish and strengthen" bodies, when I know I'm about to load them full of nitrates because it's the only food they'll ingest. Now is when I worry about such things because every other mother in a 4,723-mile radius is getting their precious little ones to eat organic, locally-sourced vegetarian lasagnas, after which their kids practice masterpieces on two different instruments, followed by an hour spent corresponding with pen-pals in developing nations.

Now is when I need my mom to say, "That isn't even happening. Quit being Type A. Chicken nuggets for dinner every day only kills people without access to cholesterol medicine. Relax."

Looking forward to someday doesn't help there. My kids will all be dead of chicken nugget heart attacks by the time I get to ask my mom, "What should I do?" So I don't look to the future for stuff like that. Sometimes, though, I look to the past, because I imagine the one thing my mom would say most often to me as I parent now is, "They'll turn out all right. You did."

I did. "All right" was a long-haul destination, but I made it. I'm here despite the fact that my parents made a billion mistakes. That's reality. No one does it right all the time.

My mom wasn't a perfect mother. I understand that more as I grow as a parent. I see all the deficiencies in my education. She didn't teach me good housekeeping. She taught me even less about `cooking. And she often buried herself in books or work when home was hard, which it often was. I was a strong-willed child, and there were times she took the easy route and let me parent myself in my adolescence. I blame her totally for my refusal, to this day, to eat cooked vegetables.

But I would give much to have her back so I could hear her say, "You're doing a good job as a mother. And the vegetable thing aside, you turned out okay. Your kids will be fine."

The rest of my life would be fun to show her—my professional successes as a writer and a blogger. But those things don't matter. I may lose interest or change focus or abandon any of those roles along the way.

Motherhood is forever. And that's a really long haul. I am certain daily that I'm screwing it up. A raised voice (mine), an impatient brush off (me again), job abandonment in favor of activities that don't slime me with snot (yep, still me). Each of these small failures always feels bigger than the consistent successes.

That's when I need my mom to stand back and say, "I see the whole of you. I see the bigger picture of what you're accomplishing with these children. You are doing well. More importantly, you are doing good. Hang in there."

My husband tells me often that I'm a good mother. Unprompted. I love that. And I need it. His assurances comfort me; they matter most because we are blessed to be yoked together in raising these three kids.

But our experiences as parents are different. We are divinely designed for this to be true. What we are created and called to do within this family is different in key respects for each of us. He manages his end of things with the same jaw-dropping aptitude he shows for everything he tackles. And I show the same pattern in mothering that I do in everything else: one long string of inadvertent comedy touched every now and then by moments of grace.

When he says, "You're such a good mom," I'm learning to hug him and say thank you instead of pointing out all the ways I'm screwing it up. It helps.

But I still find myself looking for a mother. Is it in the aunt who calls to check up on me? Is it in the mother-in-law who works so very hard to respect my boundaries? Is it a neighbor lady? A friend from church?

I never find her. I do find friends who make me feel normal. Sometimes the greatest gift you can give a despairing mother is the following statement: "Don't worry. My kids do that, too." It automatically makes us feel less alone. And when I don't have someone to say that, I dredge up a memory, sometimes ancient and yellowed, sometimes only remembered through a photograph or story oft-repeated, of me rolling around in the spilled guts of a #10 can of flour, or tossing a plate of peas to the floor, or wandering out of my mom's bathroom with makeup smeared all over my face from my illicit visit to her cosmetics bag.

Even when I don't remember her reaction in that moment, I do remember two things: first, at some point, it became a story she told and laughed at often, and second, I turned out okay. So when one of my kids does the same thing, I take a deep breath, and I remind myself that yes, maybe I yelled, and maybe that guilty kid cried, but he or she is still standing. That's its own kind of victory, and I think, Since I didn't kill them, I must have only made them stronger.

And then I collect myself and start the work again of moving together toward Someday, when I will introduce them—my mother to the grandchildren she never met—and say, "I listened when you taught me. I tried to teach them." And then she will smile and look around Someday and say, "I guess you were right. We made it."

"A man sooner or later discovers that he is the master-gardener of his soul, the director of his life."

James Allen

Reaping the Benefits

Becca Wilhite

I love the idea of gardening. My dad is a champion gardener, and I have decades-worth of weeding memories, eating the warm-tomato memories, corn-shucking-on-the-run memories, overwhelming zucchini harvest memories, and random other garden memories, including the time a snake slithered right over that foot. (It wasn't my foot. But I remember the skin-crawl as though it was.)

I inherited a lot of traits from my dad, including, but not limited to, freakish memory, long phone calls, and a love for cheese and red meat. But I didn't get the green thumb, which occasionally makes me sad. I try. Often. I spend way more money on plants and garden-y stuff than I ever save on edible produce.

This year I let myself off the hook. I didn't plant anything. In fact, in the spirit of honesty, I'll tell you that I haven't actually managed to weed the garden yet. But. I have a couple of volunteers. We're eating a lot of chives, because they come back. Over and over.

Yay! And their flowers are so beauteous. We're using chives where normally we'd use green onions, and everyone's pretty glad about it. Also, the lettuces I planted last spring but which never grew? Surprise! They're coming up now. So hooray for the surprise benefits.

Yesterday at church, Brother Bob asked us if we wanted any spinach. Um, hello? Yes! So we went over there, and he cut off a bunch of gorgeous greenies, and I ooh-ed and aah-ed over his growing things, and he whacked off a bunch of rhubarb for us. I told him to leave the leaves on, because I had to go all Miss America pageantry and wave to the kids while holding this incredible bouquet of rhubarb. We went home thinking how grateful we were that we could reap the benefits of someone else's work.

Thanks, Brother Bob.

So this morning I made a pie. A strawberry-rhubarb pie. I haven't had one of those in at least 25 years. And it made me miss my mom like very few things do these days. I don't know if my mom loved-loved strawberry-rhubarb pie, but she made it, and I ate it with her. She would have been proud of my pastry today, you know. It was a thing of beauty, if I do say so myself.

We just cut into the pie, and besides me only Kid 1 ate her whole piece, and she laughed and said, "Well, Mom, you and I can eat this pie."

And my heart was happy-sad, and I wished again that Mom were here to know my kids. Because she'd think they're delightful, I guarantee it. She'd crack up at Kid 3's sense of humor. She'd be jealous of her hair, too. She'd swoon over Kid 2's Vivaldi abilities. And she'd snuggle up with her in a blanket on the couch. She'd answer all of Kid 4's questions, even when she knew he was only asking to keep her talking. She'd practice his duets with him, too, because she had the skills. She'd hold her hands together over her heart when she saw Kid 1 sing on stage, I know it. She'd practice songs with her, and help her work through tricky harmonies. And she'd pretend to be amazed at all the kid-ly braininess, when, really, she'd pretty much expect it.

And every day, when I work on this Mom business, and sing songs to my kids, and read them books (with the voices) and bite my tongue when the unkind/impatient/snarky remark wants to escape, and when I say, "B-flat, b-flat," and cook meals, I'm reaping the rewards of her seed-planting.

Thanks, Mom.

Laying Up Food Against The Season

By Karen Burton

One Fall day my youngest son, who was still at the age where he loves to do any chores that get him close to Mom and Dad, went to the back of our yard to pick all of the apples he could reach from our apple trees. We are the natural kind of gardeners (meaning, if it happens to grow without any real assistance from us we will surely pick it and eat it), and I must admit that every time we go to harvest from our two apple trees I just hope that there will be enough healthy fruit to get my ten year-old excited. We were pretty ecstatic when he came in with a big bucket of about 50 apples. So he and I spent the bulk of the afternoon canning apple pie filling.

I have often wondered about the term "laying up food against the season." There aren't any fruits or vegetables where I live that grow year-round. There is something very earthy about our natural internal clocks that let us know when it is time to store something up, so that we can have it when we might need it. When it is not seasonally available. We snatch up the strawberries in late summer when we get a good price and we freeze them or make jam. We make salsa once those tomatoes and peppers are ready. I always listen to the wise older women in my neighborhood who have this whole thing down to a science. They are like walking almanacs with all of their instincts and predictions about food. Storing it. Getting good buys on it.

That day, as I pulled the last bottles out of their bath, I sat down at the computer in our kitchen and had the strongest yearning to track down two old friends I knew back in Virginia, before I came out to Utah and stayed west. One of these friends I had not talked to or seen for eighteen years, and the other maybe ten years. No contact at all since our last meetings, not because of a falling out. Life just kept moving. I felt like I was having a physical prompt, like the knot in my stomach was a sign that I needed to find these people. Within fifteen minutes searching online I was able to track them both down and work that knot right out.

I am not too sappy about most things, but when it comes to people I am a sentimentalist. I need people. I need family, and I need people who knew me when. I feel the importance of keeping track of people in my life. Knowing where they are living, knowing about their children. This is also laying up food against the season. I need to save them up and do whatever is necessary to preserve them. Careful preparation and all the right ingredients. Screw the lid on tight, just in case I need them later. Which I will.

The Heart Has Its Language

Annette Lyon

I was ten years old, standing in a hallway with my father on the first day of class. This wasn't like any other first day of school I'd experienced. It was in a foreign country with a language I didn't speak. My father was the new mission president over the Finland Helsinki mission for the Church. That meant my family had relocated for the next three years.

The call made sense; not only was my father a former Finnish missionary, but he was a linguist with Finnish as his specialty, and he taught a Finnish literature course—in Finnish. Mom was born and raised in Helsinki. They made a great pair as missionary leaders.

All well and good and perfectly logical, but I'd just left my home, my friends, and everything familiar to me. Now I stood outside a classroom with a swarm of other ten-year-olds, unable to understand a word they said. We always spoke English at home; Mom and Dad reserved Finnish for secret conversations about Santa and groundings, so I knew nothing of the language.

Before we came here, we did have a few Family Home Evenings where we kids learned some Finnish terms—"Where's the bathroom?" and "chocolate" being the most important. Going to public school, however, was an entirely different proposition. Dad pulled out his linguistics knowledge and assured me that at my age, my brain was still malleable enough to pick up another language. Somehow his opinion wasn't all that comforting in the face of the class bully deciding he wanted to beat up the new American girl at recess. (The bully's twin sister intervened, which was the start of my first inter-language friendship.)

The first several months were hard, even with the help of a boy in class, Christopher, who'd lived in Ireland, where his mother was from, so he knew English. I don't think he appreciated his new assignment. Sitting next to a girl and acting as her interpreter wasn't cool, except for the time he happily translated for some boys who hoped I'd believe that the stuff on my lunch plate was ant eggs. I assured them—through Christopher—that I knew what rice looked like, thanks.

I stayed after school for language lessons with my teacher, Mr. Hämäläinen. When I didn't understand what was going on or what people wanted, which was often, I struggled to hold back tears. I walked home from the bus stop day after day with a brain so tired I could hardly think straight.

As Dad predicted, I did pick up the language. After some time, I became pretty much fluent, even if I retained a slight American accent. Mom and Dad encouraged us kids to speak in Finnish at home. I balked at the idea, protesting that after a full day of Finnish at school, I needed time to rest my brain and just speak English.

Truth be told, at that point, I was past the brain-fatigue stage; Finnish wasn't hard anymore, and I got along just fine at school. No, I was simply self-conscious. The idea of speaking it to Mom and Dad felt embarrassing and weird.

Dad warned me that eventually, if I didn't speak Finnish regularly when we returned to the States, I'd forget it.

Sure, Dad. I'll forget how to walk, too, I thought. Finnish was a hard-won skill, but I owned it. I assured my parents that when we returned to the States, then I'd speak to them in Finnish.

During our time in Helsinki, I went from child to teenager. The Stockholm Temple was dedicated, and our family had the opportunity to go to Sweden to attend the event. Shortly after that, I turned twelve, left Primary, and entered the Young Women program.

Back then, I would have said that the biggest influences in my life were school and my classmates. I had a paper route with several girlfriends, and I hung out with Katri and Mia regularly.

I didn't have the full picture, and I wouldn't for another twenty years.

While attending the Marjaniemi Ward, I learned the Young Women Theme—which was, at the time, a brand new concept from Church headquarters—in Finnish. I went on temple trips with the youth to Sweden, where I did proxy baptisms—in Finnish. I read scriptures—in Finnish. I sang hymns—in Finnish. I went to church and heard sermons and lessons and testimonies—in Finnish. I heard my parents bear witness to the gospel, teach and support missionaries, and comfort Church members—in Finnish.

We returned to the States the summer before I entered eighth grade. Middle-school years are miserable enough without having to change languages again, on top of having to make new friends, figure out a new school, and go through puberty all at the same time. It was rough.

I think that was my excuse for not speaking Finnish at home.

Again, Dad was right; my ability gradually faded, until one day in high school, someone joked about another person not even knowing how to say "hello" in a language they were supposedly fluent in.

In a panic, I tried to remember what the formal word for "hello" was in Finnish—and grasped at mental straws. I knew the informal "hi," but what was "hello"? My eyes watered. I was losing one of my greatest treasures—assuming I hadn't lost it already.

Many years later, after I married and had children, Mom and Dad received another calling. A brand new temple had been completed in Helsinki, and it was about to be dedicated. My parents were called as the first president and matron. In some ways, I wasn't all that surprised; when I'd heard in general conference years before that a temple would be built there, I'd privately wondered if they'd be called to preside over it at some point.

But the timing wasn't something I was crazy about. They'd just spent nearly two years in Israel at the BYU Jerusalem Center. I wanted my parents back. I wanted my kids to have their grandparents. Now they'd be gone another three years.

One consolation was that the dedicatory services were broadcast via satellite to the Conference Center in Salt Lake City, which we could attend. Mom and Dad returned from Israel for just enough time to rake leaves, repack for a much cooler climate, kiss grand-kids good-bye, and fly out again, so they missed the Finnish cultural celebration the members put on. They arrived just in time for the dedication.

At the broadcast, I found my older sister at the Conference Center, and our families sat together. Then we watched the dedication on a screen. There was the gorgeous celestial room. There was President Hinckley, our prophet. And, there! I made out the backs of Mom's and Dad's heads—and was suddenly glad they both had distinct hairstyles, Dad with his distinguished graying swoop, Mom with a blonde French roll.

The speakers paused regularly for the Finnish interpreter. As the meeting went on, I understood more and more of the Finnish—and even thought of alternate translations. I was remembering. The dedicatory prayer moved me to tears. By the end, I was a quiet, yet sobbing mess.

The experience was overwhelming, but I puzzled at myself—it surely didn't warrant this level of tears. Yes, I would miss my parents, but I'd just seen them the other day; I didn't miss them yet.

Why was I crying so hard? Why had my heart been so deeply pricked? Why did my chest felt as if a fire burned inside it?

As the services ended and we walked out, I noticed my older sister with eyes as red as my own. She came up to me and wrapped me in a tight embrace. Then she whispered in my ear.

"You and I had some of our earliest and most powerful spiritual experiences over there. A part of our hearts can be touched only by Finnish."

I clung tighter to her and nodded. Yes. That's why I was feeling the Spirit so strongly.

I thought of the early experiences that had built my testimony. I hadn't realized how big a role Finnish had played. During each of those events, I'd been in Finland, surrounded by Finnish, whether spoken or written. I heard testimonies born from the pulpit and felt the power of the speakers' faith in their words. As a young woman, I had leaders teach me lessons about Jesus Christ. All in Finnish.

Yes, I forgot a lot of the language I once knew.

But my heart never did.

So the moment I was in a deeply spiritual situation and I heard Finnish again, my soul opened up. I felt closer to God than I had in years. I wept.

Afterward, I decided to get my Finnish back, and to do so through my faith. I began reading the Book of Mormon—aloud—in Finnish. At first the words were foreign; I felt like that ten-year-old coming home from school with brain exhaustion.

Now, the more I read, the more I understand, and the more that same old part of my heart—the piece that can be pricked solely by the beautiful language of my other home country—swells, and my faith is strengthened.

I think back on the girl I once was, sitting with Mr. Häämäläinen as he pointed to a picture of a marker and said, "Tussi."

I'd like to whisper in that girl's ear to keep working on it. Don't give up, even though yes, it's a hard language. It'll be worth it. One day, you'll stand and repeat words with other young women:

Me olemme Taivallisen Isän tyttäriä. Hän rakastan meitaä, ja me rakastamme Hänta.

And you'll know you speak truth.

The English version would one day be sweet in its own way:

We are daughters of our Heavenly Father, who loves us, and we love Him.

But the Finnish would always capture my heart and bring tears to my eyes.

No, the word for marker would never be critical to feeling my Savior's love.

Learn as much of the language as you can anyway, I'd tell myself. The better you understand it—with all its crazy endings—the more you'll feel God's love.

The greater my faith would grow. The greater my conviction that Heavenly Father knows me personally.

"Sinä olet Hänen tyttärensä," I'd say.

"You are His daughter."

Eve and Me

Cari Banning

Just as I was wrapping up grad school, I was offered a job teaching Spanish at a private school in California. While I very much enjoyed my colleagues there, I could tell that my belief system was accepted but not necessarily admired.

Two months into the school year, I was assigned to chaperone the newly-minted ninth-grade class on a trip to Yosemite National Park. Each day, out among the trees, there were various team-building activities designed to help the students get to know each other better. One chilly morning, another chaperone, Rob, and I participated in a fast-paced game where the two of us and a couple of very short 14-year-olds found ourselves in a group hug. There was a brief moment when Rob's eyes met mine—and then, suddenly, he dashed off to another group hug. During that nanosecond-long meeting, there was an indescribable impression—it was gone almost before I was aware of its presence—but it hinted at some kind of connection between Rob and me.

As I got to know him over the next couple of years, I found that he was unaffected by—even uninterested in—my beliefs. He was agnostic. Rob was one of those rare people who treats everyone as equals. He was as playful as a two-year-old and as careful as an eighty-two year old; he was both childlike and refined, a rare combination. His naturally curly hair, affable nature, and impish grin made him not just approachable, but an instant friend of people of all ages, especially children. His intent gaze and earnest expression made everyone feel as though they had his undivided attention.

Rob and I became good friends. Besides teaching, he coached soccer. He was one of my best resources when I was learning how to be a good cross-country coach. No matter what we did, we always had fun together. Once, after indulging in some Baskin-Robbins, we decided to leave our empty ice cream containers on a compulsively-neat friend's front porch. We dropped them there, rang the doorbell and ran. We were in our thirties, and we couldn't stop laughing as we sped away like a couple of reckless teenagers.

However, my own teenage years were far less light-hearted. This freedom and playfulness almost felt like the do-over I'd always wished for. When I was fourteen, I received my patriarchal blessing. It said that the spirituality in my own home would largely depend on me. That direction was ever-present in the back of my teenage mind and definitely influenced some big decisions.

The weight of it was intensified at fifteen, when I did some investigating and discovered that my Dad had left the church. Separation and divorce ensued three years later, turning my life upside-down. I felt isolated and abandoned. Those traumatic events pushed me out of "the norm." Ever since then I have felt as though I live on the edge, in the periphery, on the margin. I find that I can live there and be relatively comfortable, as long as I have my spirituality anchored.

Since those traumatic events in my teens, some of the questions I've had have been so unique to my own circumstances, that I have needed more divine guidance than some might expect. Thankfully, sometime in my childhood I learned that every answer could be found in the scriptures. Maybe it was back in mid-week Primary, which I loved to attend even though I hated wearing a dress. Or maybe it was during early-morning seminary, when my dad would wake me with an all-too-vigorous back rub "to get my blood flowing" so I'd be ready when my ride arrived. What stayed with me is that someone opened my mind to the truth that the scriptures are always there for me. I turn to them often.

At twenty, partly in response to the earlier direction from my patriarchal blessing, I decided to go on a mission. I came away with a fierce determination to marry another returned missionary in the temple.

Gradually I found myself in a complex situation as my friend, Rob, and I progressed toward a dating relationship. Early on in our friendship, we had a conversation in which Rob explained to me his objections to organized religion. Toward the end of the conversation he made it clear that it would be over his dead body that he would join any church, let alone the Mormon Church. That didn't bother me one bit since I felt that it would be pretty much over my dead body that I would marry outside the temple. After many years of a wonderful friendship and an on-again, off-again courtship, I realized that during the on-again phases, I was hard-pressed to be at peace. I definitely wanted to raise a family in the light of the gospel of Jesus Christ. I just didn't see how that could happen with Rob. I concluded that our relationship wasn't going to work, so we went our separate ways.

I was 35 at the time and had made my peace with being single – and expected to remain that way for the rest of my life. I felt I had everything I needed to be happy in my circumstances.

However, just before I ended the relationship with Rob, I had an unforgettable dream about having to give birth upside-down. It had a profound and unsettling impact on me. I recognized that its significance was deeper than I could comprehend at that time. In hindsight, I am convinced that the dream was preparatory to spiritual events to come.

One day, ten months later, Rob popped into my mind and I couldn't get him out, despite the success I'd had trying to forget him over the previous months. Not only was he on my mind, but there was an overwhelming impression that accompanied my thoughts of him. It was that a marriage relationship with him could, would and should work. I walked around in this state for several days, my mind and my heart nearly exploding, not saying a word to anyone about it, trying to figure out where this was coming from. At a certain point I was able to discern that this was, indeed, revelation from my Heavenly Father. I typically had no problem doing His will, but because this was outside the lines—this was an exception to the rule—I really wanted, and needed, a deeper understanding, which I ultimately found in the scriptures.

Over time, I was drawn to the story of Eve. I understood to my core that her choice was not whimsical. It was not made in a moment of weakness. It became obvious to me that she had a paradigm shift. Eve must have been mulling that "be fruitful, multiply, and replenish the earth" command over and over in her mind, trying to figure out how to obey. It occurred to me that I, too, would have to go down a road that differed from my initial understanding. That gave me the courage to marry Rob.

The Eve Paradox is also, for me, the Eve Paradigm—the evidence is overwhelming that as she made that decision, she carefully weighed not only her own future, but also that of generations to come. Although it looks to some like she strayed from the path, she never stopped moving in the right direction.

While some may believe that I've strayed from the path, I feel like Eve did--I am glad, because had I not made the choice to marry him I never would have had my children--who are my heart--and never would have known the soul-enlarging vicissitudes of marriage and family life.

My husband still has his same objections to organized religion. But he has a deep respect for my faith because it has made me who I am. It is that esteem for me that brings him to church every Sunday so that we can be together as a family in sacrament meeting. He makes sure he is available for family prayer. He prays with our children when I'm not there so that they will experience the consistency they need. He makes time for Family Home Evening, and is sensitive to my faith as we make decisions in their upbringing. However, all these things are merely procedure for him, some of them hollow. If I dwell on that thought for too long, I start to feel like I'm slipping down a steep hill, grasping for a handhold. He has no faith, but he does have a tremendous moral construct of his own design. He has no priesthood, but he does have a vision of a united and loving family. We don't have the kind of marriage I expected, but we are consistently blessed beyond what I had imagined when I made the decision to marry Rob.

As my little ones grow, I feel the awesome responsibility for the spirituality in our home, just as my patriarchal blessing indicated. Sometimes this is overwhelming. For now, it's up to me, alone, to guide my family in faith. I often think of Adam and Eve, together, teaching everything they learned to their children. I had always looked forward to spiritual intimacy with my spouse. I don't have that, and I long for it.

As I continue on this peripheral path, I return often to Eve's story. I find comfort and encouragement there. I need both because, at times, I find myself tempted to ask if I did the right thing. But the questions stop there because, ten years into it, I wouldn't trade what we have for a mainstream LDS family. I like to think that we are trail blazers. I find it amusing that we live on the edge of the ward and stake boundaries--it parallels our life perfectly. To be sure, sometimes I resist this often more-difficult path. I'm not naturally drawn to paradox. Nevertheless, I remain convinced that, like Eve, God wanted me to do the "wrong" thing for a more right reason. I'm so glad that after one difficult upside-down in my life, a second upside-down twenty years later ended up setting things nearly right side-up.

In the Shadow of the Colossus

Gideon Burton

I used to play *Shadow of the Colossus* with my son, Adam. It's a Sony Playstation game set in a *Lord-of-the-Rings*-type fantasy world where you have to fight a series of monsters against the backdrop of an entrancing soundtrack. It was a way to spend time with him when I had no time as a bishop. I would sit in the blue BYU banana chair in our darkened basement with him and take the controller. Adam would coach me on how to climb up the shaggy back of some agile, furry beast and hold on for dear life until I could make my way to that vulnerable place behind his skull and jab it repeatedly with my dagger. It was hard. I would sweat and tense up. It was, as my teens say, "epic."

> *For we wrestle not against flesh and blood, but against principalities, against powers, against the rulers of the darkness of this world, against spiritual wickedness in high places.*

Now, there's some New Testament drama for you. I have to admit I love this passage from Paul's letter to the Ephesians in part because it just sounds so cool. There it is: Christian salvation as a dramatic battle -- and just listen to the rhythm in this phrase: "the rulers of the darkness of this world" -- epic!

But most our lives are not. No special effects, no John Williams soundtrack. The monsters are more metaphorical, and the furry beasts are more like this rabbit that sits on my chest as I type. Cute little thing. This is not some hell-beast with fangs and claws that I must face in single combat on a foggy plain. No, this is a diminutive, American-Polish bunny with oh-so-soft, steel-grey fur. His name is not Grendel; it's "Danno."

Danno is the first of a team of rabbits we are going to be acquiring that will be named after Hawaii Five-O characters, I am told by Karen. I think she's serious, and I'm trying to remember how many characters starred in that show. We used to watch Hawaii Five-O reruns on a fuzzy black and white TV in our tiny Provo apartment when we were newly married 25 years ago. Now, with our nest starting to empty, Karen has begun gathering and breeding small animals.

We already had a dog, but one day Karen picked up "Chachi," a tiny terrier-chihuahua mix who would keep company with Bravo, our brown-coated choodle (chihuahua-poodle). These are inside/outside dogs that live mostly in our sun room in the back. On good behavior they are occasionally allowed into the main floor of the house. Will we never learn? Earlier this week, right after I let them roam into the kitchen area, Chachi peed on my new leather coat that I'd left on the floor. It wasn't that Chachi fouled my clothing;

it was that he was looking over his shoulder at me while doing it. There was swearing, and there was chasing, and there was a casting out of demons in a rather literal manner. One of our teens recently accused his parents of getting small animals so we could have more things to yell at. In all honesty, I had no idea how to answer him.

As I've been typing here on the laptop, Danno has been padding his way around the leather couch next to me, far quieter than the two teens scrounging lunch in the kitchen. "You are the biggest hypocrite in all the land. Admit it!" says one of the Shining Youth of Zion to his brother as something overcooks in the microwave. A moment later they are singing a song together: "the roots grow down and the plants grow up." Ten seconds later they are fighting over cheese. "You can't just take what's in my bowl!" I love those two.

Danno nibbles at my laptop cord. I pause to gauge how serious he is, remembering how a prior dog, Crenshaw, had chewed clean through our TV cable one year, creating an additional layer of madness during March Madness. If things continue at their present rate, when those two leave the house in another five or six years, I anticipate an entire menagerie with goats and llamas and an emu for good measure. We will have to move from Hawaii Five-O characters to a larger pool of names, like the MoTabs. Right now Karen is off at IFA getting hay for her critters. Danno has just pebbled the couch with rabbit tracks. Easy cleanup. No swears.

This morning we attended the funeral for Harriet Strong. Harriet was described in the funeral as someone with a great WQ, a "wonder quotient." She was consulting her 1950s World Book Encyclopedia as recently as last week, and she would phone her daughter in town and tell her to get outside and take a good look at the beautiful sunset.

Wonder Quotient. I love that. And I wonder if I've modeled to my sons enough of that sort of raw, divine, primal, unqualified awe at the glories of the natural world. It's why I want to take my third son skiing this season out in God's back yard. But the boys are asking for *Call of Duty 3* to feed their video addictions, rather than a telescope.

The two teens are in the living room with me now, and Danno is back in his own space. North Carolina State is kicking Clemson's butts, and I realize that I am genuinely interested, stopping my writing to cheer on the boys in red -- about whom I know nothing and care less. Karen has taught me to root for all underdogs. Clemson is ranked 7th, and NC State is unranked, and there is such a high to seeing the crowd rise with the accelerating score. I'm not a sports guy. Karen is the sports guy in our family, so I laugh at myself for having achieved the state of cheering for a team I don't know.

After I was released as bishop in 2010 I had a glorious four months as the Primary pianist. Then all that new media I've been integrating into my English classes at BYU caught up with me, and I found myself part of a pilot mission housed at the Mission Training Center. Disabled or injured missionaries, otherwise worthy and ready to serve, teach people online full time for 24 months. So in my current calling I teach missionaries how to blog.

Of course, blogging is a small part of what the online missionaries do. They take inbound live chats from Mormon.org, 'friend' investigators and members on Facebook, and conduct lessons via Skype, the phone, and even text messaging. This is the future of Mormon proselyting, and it's pretty exciting stuff. Elder Spencer with his leukemia, Elder Sabin with his cystic fibrosis, Elder

Meza with his messed up knee, Elders Callahan and Corbett with spina bifida -- and every single week their investigators (literally from the four corners of the globe) become members of our faith, having been drawn both to the Church of Jesus Christ and to this new medium. Four hundred have already joined through online instruction in almost three years.

One of the more conventional missionaries serving in Mexico right now is our second son, Elder Adam Burton. Our first son, Perry, served in Kenya. Our third son, a sophomore taking American Sign Language, is imagining a mission among the deaf. Missions are so embedded into the Mormon way of life. Just now, my third son's friend, Ian, has come over and somehow he has brought up his father's mission to Tennessee. He is graphically describing how his dad ate squirrel brains. "They just pop the head off and boil it, then peel the fur off later, crack the skull, and eat the brains." Karen is squirming, but that's the sort of hardcore folklore that will get Ian adventuring on his own mission in a few years. Look at how he talks about it.

We all do this. I once drove my family to Montreal and to the Jewish bagel shop where the best sesame bagels in the world are sold. They know about me living in the former nunnery, and ice skating on parking lots following ice storms, and then there was all that religious part of my mission, too, of course.

Karen and I think about a future mission, perhaps to the land of her ancestors in Portugal. But for now, our mission focus is on Monterrey, Mexico. Adam's been gone 18 months, and we miss him very much.

Adam has a wonder quotient. Before his mission he used

to take pictures of clouds with his cell phone. This pleased me. I don't think you can be very far off the mark if you are looking up in wonder at God's cotton candy. He still takes such photos -- lots of them -- occasionally annoying his parents because he appends to his email not photos of a healthy, happy missionary son but yet another set of shots of Cerro de la Silla, "Hill of the Saddle," the mountain that dominates the large Mexican metropolis of Monterrey like Diamond Head does Honolulu. He never tires of it, or of golden hour images of a nearby river or path. Harriet would be proud.

Playing *Shadow of the Colossus* seems so long ago now, like those Hawaii Five-O reruns that Karen and I watched in our first Provo apartment, 25 years before she was naming this rabbit "Danno." Time does that to you. Parents start to know just how fleeting time is with their little ones. And now our red head turns 21 in a couple of weeks and his girlfriend is serving a mission in Berlin and I am thinking back even further in time to when I put Adam on one knee, Perry on another, and each of us pressed one key on the computer keyboard as we fought aliens together. Am I getting nostalgic about playing video games with my kids? I am.

I got a private letter from Adam the other week, right as I was missing him most. He told me he and his companion were walking down a busy street in Monterrey and he stepped on a scratched up CD lying in the street. "But it wasn't a CD, Dad. It was a game disk. It was *Shadow of the Colossus!* Remember when we played that together?"

Yes, I remember.

We live in the shadow of a colossus, the beast of time that takes children from us and replaces them with avatars of who they were. Replaces us with avatars of who we were. And pretty soon, the son you fought aliens with while bouncing him on your knee is married and not returning your emails, while Chachi is squatting on your leather coat while you make dinner for two.

At the funeral today, Harriet's children, in their 70s, remarked on how their mother was always reading. What will our children remember about Karen and me when we go? Today I made the two teens watch me in the kitchen as I kissed their mother and hugged her tightly. "Watch and learn," I commanded, much as my own father had done while similarly smooching Mom in their kitchen years ago. Then I snapped a photo of Karen holding Danno while one of our sons grimaced. I titled it "Honey, bunny, and sonny" and posted it to Facebook. Within a couple of hours our oldest son and his wife had both "liked" the pic. Hey, how about that? I saw it as reclaiming, just a little, what the colossus has been taking away. Not quite as satisfying as plunging a dagger twelve times into the skull of a monster, to be sure, but it will do for now.

Writing and Life

Becca Wilhite

Writing is not my life.

It is part of my life – a part that I love and crave and enjoy.

But Living, that's my life.
Working and playing and eating and cooking
and praying and reading and studying and serving and singing and
rejoicing
and loving
and laughing and crying
and exercising
and struggling
and even cleaning (sometimes)
and driving all over town
and moving across the living room with the sunspot in the afternoon.

And putting words on the pages.

Lots of words.

Sometimes bribing myself to stay in the chair,

Just two hundred more words.

Just one thing that makes you laugh.

Just one more hour.

Then you can have the thing you've been waiting for.

And other times,

magic times,

losing hours in the dance of creation.

And remembering that if I'm a writer,

I am also so many other things.

So many -ers.

And those things, those labels, those actions

and thoughts

and attempts,

and the ME that grows out of them,

and the love

and all those living parts,

That's what I can write about.

Every day.

It's in the Telling

Gideon Burton

I t's in the telling, telling who I am.
  It's in the fashioning, rough-hewn and raw
and wrought in work'day wonder, awkward awe,
misgiving and yet living in a land
of little certain, more that's deep and grand.
Yet in my splintered stumbling kick and cough
toward that center hidden, thrown aloft,
it's who I am in telling, that I am.
Committed (as a patient, athlete, priest)
a smith of time, a mimic, bard, or child
performing words whipped tame (more often, wild)
to press for most while host to what seems least:
  I speak, I write, undone with each revision;
  remade reworked, revived in storied vision.

AUTHORS

Cari Banning is a stay-at-home mom who adores her family, loves the outdoors and finds housework vexing. She earned her B.A. and M.A. in Spanish Linguistics from BYU. She is a teacher by profession. Cari, her husband and two children are natives of Los Angeles, CA, where they happily reside. (**193**)

Josh Bingham studied English and creative writing at Brigham Young University. He recently returned to his home state of Utah after spending a few years in Portland, Oregon. When not writing, Josh works in retail management and loves reading, cooking and spending time with his three children and beautiful wife. You can find him blogging online with his writing buddies Ken Craig, Patrick Livingston, and Chris Clark at www.parttimeauthors.com (**47, 115**)

Michelle Budge received a BFA in Interior Design from Brigham Young University and a BFA in Advertising from Art Center College of Design. A short essay she wrote received a One Club scholarship for copywriting from Art Center College of Design. She once drove an International Harvester combine for a summer job, but is now a Graphic Designer working in Los Angeles. In addition to more than fifteen years' experience designing marketing and communication materials for large corporations, Michelle has provided 15+ years of marketing and communication design for multiple LDS ward and stake activities. She is the favorite "Aunt Michellie" of ten perfect nieces and nephews. She also designs her own line of prints and posters; TYPE TYPE TYPE featuring inspirational quotes, scriptures and teaching aids for LDS Young Women, Relief Society, Seminary and Primary. TYPE TYPE TYPE prints and posters are available online at typetypetype.etsy.com. (**91**)

Gideon Burton teaches English and new media at Brigham Young University, and has recently advised a pilot program for online proselyting. In addition to teaching students and missionaries how to blog and use social media, he has co-authored (with Monica Blume) the book, *For the Love of a Child: The Journey of Adoption*, and has composed hundreds of sonnets (see opensourcesonnets.blogspot.com). He is married to Karen Burton, and they are the parents of four sons. (**199, 208**)

210

Karen Burton has been blogging since 2008, finding it a rewarding outlet to ponder the commonplace of a busy and happy life. Inspired by the everyday, Karen writes about her faith, her job as a special education teacher, and raising a family. Her blog, "Kazzy's Ponderings," is found at www.kazzysponderings.blogspot.com. (**147, 184**)

Christopher Clark was raised in Provo UT, and received a bachelor's degree in English and a Ph.D in Education Leadership from Brigham Young University, as well as an MFA degree in Directing Shakespeare from Exeter University, UK. He teaches acting at Utah Valley University, and has directed plays at the Utah Shakespeare Festival, The Hale Center Theatre (Orem), The Hale Center Theatre (West Valley), and the Northcoast Repertory Theatre in San Diego. Chris and his wife Lisa have five children and live in Provo, where they meet the occasional Mormon. Chris shares a blog with his friends Ken Craig, Patrick Livingston, and Josh Bingham, at www.parttimeauthors.com (**12, 23**)

Ken Craig is a writer and business owner. He began writing comedy sketches while in college as a founding member of a university comedy troupe, where he met and married his wife. He has since written professionally for various businesses and has been published in several magazines. This is his first book. Ken serves as a bishop in the Church of Jesus Christ of Latter-day Saints in Las Vegas, Nevada, where he resides with his wife, Katie, and their seven children. Their family adventures are featured in Ken's blog, "The Craig Report," www.thecraigreport. com. Ken's writing may also be found at www.parttimeauthors.com. (**25, 53, 159**)

Debbie Frampton is a freelance writer and editor, as well as a former composition and literature instructor at BYU-Hawaii. Creative non-fiction is her genre of choice and while she has largely published articles, stories and poems of a serious nature, her forte is using humor to point out absurdity and express grief. Debbie's humor blog can be found at crashtestdummydiaries.com (**36, 165**)

DeNae Handy is an avid writer, blogger, editor, and public speaker. She published her first collection of essays in 2001, and expects to publish two more collections in

AUTHORS

2012. DeNae graduated from the University of Utah with a degree in music, and has enjoyed a career as a conductor, teacher, arranger, and orchestrator. She has also spent the better part of the last twenty years teaching institute, seminary, and adult religion classes for the LDS Church, and enjoys speaking at church conferences and other events. DeNae is the mother of four (grown or nearly grown) children, and has been married to her husband, Brett, for 27 years. Her off-beat humor infuses her blog, "My Real Life Was Backordered," at www.thebackorderedlife.com. (**2, 31, 43, 60**)

Melanie Bennett Jacobson is an avid reader, amateur cook, and champion shopper. She consumes astonishing amounts of chocolate, chick flicks, and romance novels. After meeting her husband online, she is now living happily married in Southern California with her growing family and a series of doomed houseplants. Melanie is a former English teacher and an experienced speaker who loves to laugh and make others laugh. In her down time (ha!), she writes romantic comedies for Covenant Communications and maintains her humorous slice-of-life blog at www.readandwritestuff.com. Her third novel, *Twitterpated*, hits shelves in March 2012. (**107, 174**)

Patrick Livingston is a playwright whose plays have been produced in Los Angles, New York City and Provo. He and his writing partners have written four plays and are currently in the process of completing a screenplay adaptation of their latest play. He is part of the Improvisational troupe 'The Thrillionaries' and periodically blogs at patrickandlindsayliv.blogspot.com, or with his friends Ken, Josh, and Chris at www.parttimeauthors.com. He is an adoring husband of a brilliant and talented woman and together they are raising a brilliant and talented daughter. Everything he writes is for them. (**16, 98**)

Annette Lyon is a Whitney Award winner, the recipient of Utah's Best of State medal for fiction, and the author of eight novels, a cookbook, a grammar guide, and well over a hundred magazine articles. She's a senior editor at Precision Editing Group and a cum laude graduate from BYU with a degree in English. When she's not writing,

212

editing, knitting, or eating chocolate, she can be found mothering and avoiding the spots on the kitchen floor. Find her online at blog.annettelyon.com and on Twitter: @AnnetteLyon (**80, 186**)

Jana Winters Parkin was born and raised in Salt Lake City, but spent most of her adult life in the greater Los Angeles area, which she still thinks of as 'home.' Jana attended the Otis Art Institute in Los Angeles and the University of Cambridge in England, both on scholarships awarded for essays she wrote. She graduated with a BFA from the University of Utah. Over the next 17 years she ran a successful design firm out of their house in Southern California while raising three spirited children. Then, in a sudden twist of fate, her husband Jeff accepted a teaching job at BYU and the whole family relocated to Provo, Utah. Jana took advantage of the lifestyle change to abandon the deadlines and headaches of being "designer to the rich and famous" and shifted her interest to a more peaceful regimen: painting, hiking and writing. When she's not driving carpools, she explores the trails of Provo Canyon, teaches art at Utah Valley University, exhibits her paintings throughout Utah and online at ParkinX.com, and writes at DivergentPathways.blogspot.com. In addition to *Tell Me Who I Am*, she illustrated *What Think Ye of Christmas?*, published in 2010. Jana firmly believes that the universe grants the best adventures and most exciting story-fodder to the lives of those who are willing to treasure them, collect them, and share them. (**9, 122, 126, 132, 154, 171**)

Luisa M. Perkins, a BYU graduate, is the author of *Dispirited*, forthcoming from Zarahemla Books in April 2012, and co-author of the novel *The Book of Jer3miah*, forthcoming from Shadow Mountain in August 2012. Past publications include the cookbook *Comfortably Yum* and the YA novel *Shannon's Mirror*. She has had numerous short stories and essays published in print and online. She has been a member of the Whitney Awards Committee for the past two years. She serves as the Director of the Yorktown Family History Center in the Yorktown, New York Stake. She and her husband Patrick live with their six children in New York's Hudson Highlands. (**135**)

AUTHORS

Stephanie Sorensen is the mother of three young and relentless children. She loves to study, read, and teach about the gospel of Jesus Christ. Her other interests include Latin music, naps, restaurants, writing, travel, teaching, housework denial and long showers. Stephanie seeks for the divinity in motherhood--- tries to share it when she finds it, and tries to laugh when she doesn't. She blogs her musings at diapersanddivinity.com. (**70, 88**)

Becca Wilhite is wife to one and mom to four. She writes novels for teenagers (*Bright Blue Miracle* and *My Ridiculous Romantic Obsessions*) and a blog for everyone else. She loves her opportunities to teach and lecture about writing and experiencing life. Growing up as a member of the Church of Jesus Christ of Latter-day Saints has given her ample opportunity to learn, teach, and share her beliefs by the way she lives. Find her online at www.beccawilhite.com (**65, 76, 141, 149, 181, 206**)

www.ingramcontent.com/pod-product-compliance
Lightning Source LLC
Chambersburg PA
CBHW061430040426
42450CB00007B/980